Strategic Supremacy
PURE & SIMPLE

**Don't Change The Rules,
Change The Game**

"You need to have
supremacy of *thinking*
before you can achieve
supremacy of *strategy.*"

-   Mike Robert
Founder,
Decision Processes International

Also by Michel Robert

The Strategist CEO
The Innovation Formula
Strategy Pure and Simple
Product Innovation Strategy Pure and Simple
Strategy Pure and Simple II
The Power of Strategic Thinking
e-Strategy Pure and Simple

Michel Robert is the founding partner of Decision Processes
International, a global management consulting firm which is
a pioneer in the field of critical thinking processes. These
processes, such as Strategic Thinking, Strategic Product
Innovation and e-Strategy, have helped more than 500
companies to achieve supremacy and transform the way
they do business.

Additional books may be ordered from Decision Processes
International, 10 Bay Street, Westport, CT 06880.
Telephone: 1-800-336-7685 (in CT: 203-454-1286).
Fax: 203-226-5802.
Visit DPI on the Internet at www.decisionprocesses.com

Strategic Supremacy
PURE & SIMPLE

Don't Change The Rules, Change The *Game*

Michel Robert

Founder - Partner
Decision Processes International

Published by

PPS
Poutray, Pekar, Stella, Inc.
Norwalk, CT

Robert, Michel
    Strategic supremacy pure and simple: don't change
the rules, change the game. / Michel Robert

    ISBN 0-9709985-0-3
    1. Strategic Planning – United States
2. Competition   3. Success in Business – United States
I. Title.

            Published by

            PPS
    Poutray, Pekar, Stella, Inc.
          Norwalk, CT
          203-853-4000

    1 2 3 4 5 6 7 8 9 0

ISBN 0-9709985-0-3

Books are available from Decision Processes International,
10 Bay Street, Westport, CT 06880, 1-800-336-7685,
(in CT 203-454-1286), fax: 203-226-5802.
Internet: www.decisionprocesses.com

Although the author has thoroughly researched all sources to ensure the
accuracy and completeness of the information contained in this book we
assume no responsibility for errors, inaccuracies, omissions and any other
inconsistency herein. Any slights against people or organizations are
unintentional.
Edited by William D. Poutray
Book jacket design by Dawn Smeraglino
Typesetting by Andrée Côté

To my wife Ellie, my best critic, for enduring my writing books on our honeymoon and our vacations. And to my daughters, Emma and Samantha, who I hope will be inspired to realize that achievement in life is totally unrelated to one's origin.

Strategic Supremacy
Table of Contents

PREFACE

Our firm, Decision Processes International, has been involved in the field of strategy for over 25 years. During this span of time, we have seen a multitude of so-called strategy consultants and strategic concepts come and go faster than the latest seasonal clothing fad.

To mention just a few that have come and gone since 1975, the following are some of the concepts which have landed on the strategic scrapheap.

- the concept of Stars, Dogs and Cash Cows espoused by the Boston Consulting Group
- the Diversified Portfolio concept, also espoused by the Boston Consulting Group in the 1970's
- the "S" curve theory espoused by McKinsey
- the Value Chain concept espoused by Michael Porter and the Monitor Group
- the Undiversification of Diversified Portfolios concept, again espoused by the Boston Consulting Group in the1980's
- the concept of Strategic Intent espoused by Gary Hamel in the mid-1980's
- the concept of Raising The Bar as espoused by Jack Welch of General Electric
- the concept of Balanced Scorecard espoused by Nathan Kaplan.

Many of these concepts were so "sexy" that they seduced many intelligent CEOs and their executive teams into using them only to find out sometime later that they were conceptually flawed. They were flawed because the concepts had not been validated in the real world. They emerged from books written by business school professors who studied firms from the "outside" and attempted to recreate the magic recipes that these firms were following without ever speaking to anyone at these companies. They then published a book around their so-called "findings."

At DPI, we believe that the reason our concepts of Strategic Thinking, which we first marketed in 1980, have withstood the test of time is that they were developed in a very different manner. They were developed by participating in *real strategy* meetings conducted by *real* CEOs running *real* companies. In other words, our concepts originated from the "war rooms" of some of the world's leading corporations and have been validated with more than 400 other corporations over more than twenty years.

Our Strategic Thinking Process, first introduced in 1980, contains several unique and proprietary concepts such as:

- the concept of a singular Driving Force at the root of a company's strategy
- the concept of Areas of Excellence required to assure the success of a strategy
- the concept that companies compete, not business units
- the concept of Strategic Leveraging
- the concept of managing your competitor's strategy to your advantage
- the concept of controlling the "sandbox"
- the concept of changing the rules of play

These have not only stood the test of time, but have become more robust as they have been "put to the test" around the world by the executive teams of these 400 major corporations.

Our work with our clients also allows us to detect emerging concepts *before* they become "mainstream" and before business school professors become aware of them.

This book is about such an event. Since 1980, we have counseled our clients that *"significant shifts in market share occur, not by imitating a competitor's strategy, but by developing a strategy that changes the rules of play."* This concept has worked brilliantly for many of our clients.

During this period, I have authored 8 books which contain interviews with over 50 CEOs of our client organizations which all attest to these results.

Recently, however, we have noticed a number of changes happening in the world of business that have convinced us that merely changing the rules of play will not be enough to win in the future. Our thesis, as described in the remainder of this book, is that companies which aspire for *strategic supremacy* in the future will have to *change the very nature of the game itself.*

No longer will it be enough to change the rules. It will become imperative to *reinvent the game itself,* thus enabling a company to force its competitors to play this new game according to daunting new rules.

This is what this book is all about.

Good reading!

Mike Robert

Chapter 1

Supremacy:
Not A Dirty Word

What do Intel, Wal-Mart, Home Depot, Microsoft, Dell, Apple, Oracle, CNN, Schwab, MCI Worldcom, Genentech, E-Trade, amazon.com, FedEx, Caterpillar, IBM, General Electric, Nortel, Nokia, priceline.com, Progressive Insurance, Canon, Sony, Disney, and Southwest Airlines have in common?

Let's try to answer this question through the process of elimination by first looking at what is *different* about them:

- they are in different industries
- they have different products
- they serve different customers and markets
- they have different "modus operandi"
- they are headquartered in different countries
- they cultivate different corporate cultures
- they were conceived in different eras

The list could go on *ad infinitum*. For example, another one is that they have different CEOs. However, these different companies have, or had at one point, CEOs who had one trait in common. And that trait is a grasp of the concept of *strategic supremacy*. In other words, their goal was not to have a strategy that allowed their companies to compete "adequately" but rather a strategy that aimed at *supremacy* over their competitors. *Supremacy,* not *adequacy,* is the ultimate goal of strategy.

Supremacy: The Ultimate Goal Of Strategy

Supremacy over your competitors? What an arrogant position for which to aspire! Yet, whatever one may think about the role of competition, the ultimate measure of a successful strategy is not that it allows you to compete "adequately," which is the school of management that the "best practices" strategy "gurus" have been preaching for the last thirty years. The ultimate goal of strategy should be to make competitors *irrelevant.* In fact, our view is that if you are obsessed with your competitors, it is probably because you have a "me-too" strategy that's not working and should be given a rethink. CEOs of winning companies have strategies that are *distinctive* and set them apart from their competitors. Their view of competitors is not to look sideways to see who is a "neck" ahead but rather, to periodically look *back,* to ensure that the gap is getting larger and larger. Strategic *supremacy*, not strategic adequacy, is the goal of astute CEOs. After all, history would have made short shrift of anyone named Alexander the Mediocre or Frederick the Average.

Changing The Rules

How did the companies mentioned earlier reach this elite position of supremacy? The answer: by practicing a concept of strategy that we first introduced to our clients over twenty years ago which is that the best strategy is not one that *imitates* your competitor, but rather, *changes the rules of the game!*

Imitation may be the best form of flattery, but it is the worst form of strategy. You do not distance yourself from your competitors by cloning their strategies but rather by crafting a strategy that changes the rules of the game to the extent that it allows you to *manage that competitor's strategy* as well as your own. And that is exactly what each of the CEOs of the companies mentioned above had–a strategy that changed the rules of the game.

The concept of *changing the rules of the game* is one that has stood the test of time and we have many clients who have been very successful by formulating and deploying such strategies. However, in view of a set of unique changes happening in the world today, we now believe that it is imperative to *rethink the entire process and concepts of strategy formulation and deployment.*

The Static Game Board

To date, the concept of changing the rules of the game assumed that the *game board,* upon which the competition occurred, was static. For example, the "game" of strategy can be compared to the game of chess. In chess, the game is played on a board that imposes similar rules on both players. Pawns, rooks, bishops, queens, knights and kings can only move according to a range of preset rules. As a result, both players have a *limited* number of strategies available to them to win the game and attain supremacy over their opponent. A winning strategy is constricted by the constraints (rules) that the chessboard imposes on both players equally. The same has been true in business.

Until a few years ago, each industry had a "game board" with a predetermined set of rules that were imposed on all competitors in that industry. As such, a competitor's search for a "distinctive" strategy has been limited to one confined within the constraints of the "rules" of that industry.

Disruptive Events Require A Disruptive Strategy

In the last few years, however, a number of "once in a century" changes such as biotechnology, the Internet, and the fusion of computer and telecommunication technologies are obliterating the various traditional game boards and disrupting the underlying structures of many industries.

Because these changes will alter the fundamental structures of these industries, our view is that CEOs will not only need to conceive a strategy that changes the rules of the game, but also one that will *change the nature of the game itself.* They will need to conceive a strategy that is as "disruptive" to their competitors as the changes that are disrupting the structure of the industry in the first place. Only a strategy that disrupts the status quo will result in strategic supremacy for its creator and oblige competitors who want to play to do so by abiding by rules set by that same creator. This radical departure from traditional strategy concepts provides the pathway to strategic supremacy.

FedEx: Changing The Game

There was a time not so long ago that all letters and small packages were delivered exclusively by the U.S. Postal Service, most of them within twenty-four hours. In the seventies, however, the Postal Service began to renege on that promise with mail delivery taking as long as one week. This was not ideal performance for documents that needed urgent attention. Luckily, the game was about to be changed.

Fred Smith, who had no prior knowledge of how the Postal Service operated except to know that its performance was inadequate, was searching for a topic for a paper he needed to submit in order to graduate from business school. His thesis proposed the formation of a company with a fleet of aircraft, which would fly, point to point, between major cities and a central hub in Memphis–at night! During the day, an army of small trucks would meet the planes early each morning, collect yesterday's parcels originating from all over the country, and deliver them to recipients in that city "positively, absolutely by 10:30" that morning. In the afternoons, the same trucks would collect parcels from various customers and bring them to the waiting planes that would fly them to Memphis for sorting and then dispatch them to their respective destinations.

This was a radically different concept from the way the Postal Service played the game. In fact, Smith created a brand new game. A group of investors thought Smith's concept would be so disruptive for the Postal Service that they gave him $60 million in seed capital to get his company up and running.

For years FedEx mocked and capitalized on the Postal Service's deficiencies and a full-scale war between the two emerged which went on for over 25 years. Finally, in January 2001, the mighty U.S. Postal Service capitulated. In a rare and public admission of the supremacy of FedEx's strategy, the Postal Service decided to play the game according to rules set by FedEx. It gave FedEx the largest contract it had ever awarded. The contract calls for FedEx to handle a large portion of the Postal Service's operations. Adding salt to the wound, the "treaty" also gives FedEx the right to place its own pick-up bins in every Post Office in the U.S. This could be the first step towards the eventual take-over of the Post Office by FedEx.

The graduation paper? His professor gave it a D minus! Genius is not often quickly recognized–giving strategic innovators the advantage of long lead times until their competitors gradually figure out the new game being played.

Strategic Quiz

What score would your "professor" give your current strategy?
In order to assess the degree of supremacy you have over your competitors, or that they have over you, you may wish to answer the following questions:

Does your strategy …
- correct past errors?   1
- address current conditions?   2
- exploit future trends?   3

Is your strategy …
- decreasing the gap between
  you and your competitors?   1
- keeping the gap the same?   2
- increasing the gap?   3

Does your strategy allow you to …
- control the terms of play in
  your sandbox?   1
- manage your competitor's
  business as well as yours?   2
- grow at your competitors' expense?   3

Does your strategy …

- put you on a par with your
  competitors?   1
- give you a slight edge over
  your competitors?   2
- give you a significant advantage
  over your competitors?   3
- dominate your competitors?   4
- make competitors irrelevant?   5
- eliminate competitors?   6

Total: _____

Score Interpretation

If you scored 13 or more, you already reign supreme in your sandbox. You can stop reading at this point, unless of course, you want to learn why you are doing so well. On the other hand, if you scored between 10 and 13, you are doing reasonably well but the concepts in the remainder of this book will probably help take your organization to the "next and ultimate" level of strategy.

If you scored between 6 and 9, you are good but not yet in the "major league" of strategic concepts and processes. These could turbocharge your company into the major league of business. If you scored below 6, your current strategy is not working and it's time for a major rethink.

Chapter 2

Strategic Supremacy Models

As mentioned in the Preface, "supremacy" is not an absolute percentage advantage over competitors but rather the degree of control a company has over its competitors. The thesis that we propose in this publication is that the ability to control the "sandbox" in the future has migrated from "changing the rules of play" to "changing the game itself."

There is a fine but extremely important nuance between the two concepts. The following examples are meant to illustrate that nuance.

WAL-MART

Until Wal-Mart came on the scene, the game and the rules for department store retailers were the same for all the players across the country. The game was played this way:

- Stores were located in city centers and nearby suburban areas
- The offering consisted of "dry," non-perishable goods
- Marketing was "pull" oriented
- They offered periodic sales on selected items

Wal-Mart first started by changing the rules. Contrary to the other chains that offered lower prices only on certain items each week, Sam Walton introduced the concept of "everyday low prices."

Not satisfied, Walton went even further and *changed the game itself* when he introduced several additional concepts. First, he avoided large cities and located his stores in mid-size, rural towns. Second, he clustered 10 to 12 stores around a warehouse that could replenish these stores within 24 hours. Third, he stocked the shelves with both perishable and non-perishable goods. Fourth, he instituted a program to exert severe pressure on suppliers to continuously reduce their costs and prices to Wal-Mart. The game had never been played in this manner. Sam Walton created a new game that put Wal-Mart on a path to strategic supremacy. To this day, some 40 years later, K-Mart, Sears and J.C. Penney are playing to Wal-Mart's rules and have yet to develop adequate counter-strategies. In the meantime, the gap between Wal-Mart and its competitors gets wider and wider.

amazon.com

In book selling, the game was played in a well-known manner. In order to play the game, one built a chain of stores, stocked them with as many books as could be squeezed into each store's space and then waited for people to come in, browse, and hopefully buy a book or two. Two chains, Borders and Barnes & Noble, attempted to change these rules by building stores several times larger than had been seen before, and carried over 100,000 book selections compared to 10,000 in the traditional bookstore. Furthermore, they encouraged you to browse by giving you coffee and a reading area. The new rules worked in their favor extremely well as they took more and more market share away from the operators of smaller stores. These new rules, however, were still designed for the familiar game board of "bricks and mortar."

Then along comes the Internet, and amazon.com who creates a brand new game. Amazon shuns the traditional concept of company stores–bricks and mortar–and, instead, enables you to buy books right off the Internet, offering a selection of over 1,000,000 titles at significant discounts. Furthermore, it allows you to do this from your home using your PC. Your order is confirmed while on-line and the book arrives at your door within 24 to 36 hours, all without the need to go anywhere near a bookstore. New game, no bricks and mortar, new game board–the Internet–and totally new rules set by amazon. Three years later, Borders and Barnes & Noble have yet to come up with a counter-strategy while they watch amazon establishing its supremacy over the industry.

CNN

The Network TV industry was once dominated by three networks that understood the game they were in and played by its rules. The game was established and followed in robot-like lockstep: standard broadcast capability, variety programming with kids' programs in the morning, soaps, talk and game shows in the afternoon, a news hour at dinner time, sitcoms in the evening and sports on the weekend. The three networks–ABC, CBS and NBC–understood the rules of this game so well that no one network ever gained supremacy over its two other rivals. In fact, none of the three had a distinctive strategy. They were all imitating each other with the result that, each year, they played musical chairs as to which one would get 23, 22 or 21 market share.

Ted Turner enters the game, doesn't like it, and decides to create a new game on a new game board. Instead of going standard broadcast, he goes cable and satellite. Instead of going variety programming, he goes with an all-news format. Instead of staying domestic, he goes international. Which game has established its supremacy as the premier news organization in the world and produced more wealth for its shareholders in the last 20 years? The answer: CNN, the name Turner gave to his new game. Watch for new games to emerge from this arena as satellite, cable and broadband technologies become more established worldwide.

Home Depot

For the last fifty years or so, if you were doing some repairs to your home and needed some lumber or a few 2 " screws, you would walk over to your neighborhood lumberyard and pick up a few 2 x 4's and then mosey over to Joe's hardware store to pick up the screws. Every community had its mom and pop lumberyard and hardware store and the game was played that way across America…until Arthur Blank and Bernie Marcus arrived on the scene and decided to radically change the nature of the game.

Instead of the 10,000 square foot mom and pop store, Blank and Marcus built massive, 100,000 square foot monsters that stored both lumber and hardware in quantities and varieties unseen before. To appeal to the amateur handyman, they staffed each section with a craftsman licensed in that trade which reassured the buyer that he was being served by a knowledgeable professional. Furthermore, they built hundreds of stores around the country so quickly that they established their supremacy over the mom and pop operators and other home centers that had popped up before any of them realized what hit them. When was the last time you saw the names Channel, Pergament or Builder's Square? The game was changed for good.

Roberts Express (now called FedEx Custom Critical)

There was a time in the trucking industry when the rules were the same for all the players. The basic rules were:

- Buy a fleet of trucks
- Determine whether to concentrate on short hauls or long hauls
- Hunt down customers
- Always try to get a return load from wherever you go so that you minimize empty legs
- Beat down your competitors on price which leads to razor thin margins and volatile periods of profit and losses

When the industry was deregulated in the late 70's, most trucking companies saw that event as an opportunity to extend their routes into other companies' territories. However, they continued to play the game as they did before which only led to more intense competition and even greater amounts of red ink.

The management of one company, Roberts Express, looked at the same event and saw an opportunity to change the game itself. Let's assume that you run a car assembly plant in Detroit, and you are on a JIT basis with your suppliers. Engines, for example, are delivered one shift prior to the time they are used. One day, your engine supplier has problems of his own and the engines don't show up. You are now faced with the possibility of having to shut down the plant and send 5,000 employees home.

That is when Roberts Express's strategy kicks in. Roberts has a network of 2,000 independent truck owners who identify themselves under the company's brand name located across the country waiting for your call. While you are on the phone with the Roberts dispatcher, he/she is locating, through their proprietary satellite system, the truck nearest to your engine supplier's plant. Within seconds you have a guarantee that the engines will be picked up within plus or minus 15 minutes of a specific hour and delivered to your plant within the same window also at a specific hour. This is a radically different game. On top of this, Roberts has built-in cost and flexibility advantages. Roberts doesn't own any of the trucks, thus saving a large capital expenditure that weighs down other trucking companies. The drivers, who buy their own trucks, are all independent contractors which means that Roberts has none of the administrative responsibilities that come with having those employees. But the beauty of that strategy is that Roberts gets premium prices in an industry that is renowned for cutthroat pricing. In fact, Roberts' strategy resulted in such a large "supremacy gap" over the industry that its success attracted the eye of another company that believes in strategic supremacy-FedEx. It is now a member of that family.

Southwest Airlines

Since deregulation in the early 70's, the airline industry and all its players have played the game in the same manner. All have a "hub and spoke" system; all use aircraft of different sizes and configurations manufactured by different companies; all have invested billions of dollars in sophisticated reservation systems and all continuously complain about how stupid an industry they are in with stupid competitors and even stupid customers. All…that is, except Southwest Airlines which has made a profit every day since its inception in 1972. Why? Southwest has created its own game! Instead of operating through hubs, it operates on a point-to-point basis. It floods these two locations with up to a dozen flights per day at "everyday low–and only one–price," thus drawing a multitude of first time passengers who would normally travel by bus. Instead of using multiple aircraft, it employs a single aircraft–the Boeing 737–and, as far as a sophisticated, costly reservation system…it has none! Whose strategy is quickly ascending towards supremacy over the industry? You're right. Southwest. The strategy is so far superior to the other airlines that Boeing custom built a "stretch" version of its 737 model only for Southwest. Furthermore, all of Southwest's growth has been organic whereas most other airlines' growth has been through acquisitions. For thirty years now, none of the other airlines have been able to put together a viable response to this strategy and Southwest has grown year after year at their expense.

The Body Shop

In the cosmetic industry, the game has been played by all the competitors and the rules were well known to all the players:

- Give each of your products a "brand" image
- Charge inflated prices
- Hire well-known, expensive models to endorse and promote your products
- Distribute through dedicated counter space in department stores and drugstores
- Staff these counters with your own personnel
- Use fancy packaging that frequently costs more than the product itself

Anita Roddick has built a $500 million business by changing this tired, uninspired game. Instead of marketing her products through department stores and drugstores, she sells through her own retail outlets which now number over 300 around the world. Instead of expensive packaging, Body Shop's products use plain, nondescript, recyclable materials purchased from the poorer countries of the world. In an industry that spends hundreds of millions in advertising, Body Shop doesn't even have such a budget. The strategy has been so successful that it has drawn a number of imitators who, unfortunately, are attempting to play on a game board whose rules were set and are controlled by Anita Roddick. Some traditional competitors, such as Revlon, did not even notice that there was a new game in town and, to this day, have not responded and are paying the price.

Dell Computer

Michael Dell is another individual who has built a powerhouse, multi-billion company in a few short years by first changing the rules and then by changing the game itself. Instead of marketing computers through retail stores, as the industry rules dictated back then, he decided to market PC's through direct response marketing methods. This was an attempt to change the rules which enjoyed early success. But the company's products were the same as its competitors. A few years after the company's creation, Dell decided to change the game itself. He married the concept of direct marketing with that of on-demand, made-to-order computers.

The result? A multi-billion dollar company that has the highest revenue per employee, the lowest inventory per employee, the highest return on capital and a stock price that has outperformed the market by a factor of a large scale earthquake despite the volatility of the PC market.

In 1997, Dell decided to change the game again by changing its direct marketing method from catalogues to the Internet. Only a few months after it extended this mechanism around the world, Dell was booking over $10 million in orders per day. Dell has caused other computer companies, such as Compaq, to re-think their own strategies and try to do things Dell's way. Unfortunately, they found themselves on Dell's game board whose rules are controlled by Dell. Most of its competitors have recognized the supremacy of Dell's strategy and have since given up.

Boeing's Strategic Coup

For most of this century, Boeing had established its supremacy in the aircraft design and construction sandbox. Its supremacy was so pronounced that almost all other competitors gave up and Boeing had the sandbox pretty much to itself.

That was so until a consortium of European governments decided, as an attempt to blunt Boeing's dominance, to form a company to build commercial aircraft which they named "Airbus." Airbus's strategy was very simple: "Copycat Boeing." In other words, whatever size aircraft

Boeing made, Airbus decided to duplicate it. And because Boeing was not accustomed to intense competition, Airbus eventually took 40% of the market away from Boeing.

For a while, Boeing did not know how to respond and it engaged in a battle with Airbus whereby each company attempted to outdo the other by making bigger and bigger planes. Both companies were now pursuing an "imitation" strategy, basically cloning each other. For Boeing, this was not a winning proposition. Boeing had to rethink its strategy. Finally, at the Bourget Air Show in 1999, Boeing went public with its new strategy and announced that it would build a "mega" jetliner that would carry over 800 people. It would do this by "stretching" its 747 model rather than build a brand new aircraft.

A "mega" plane had been part of Airbus's thinking as well. But Airbus had been reluctant to pursue such a gigantic aircraft because of its enormous development costs. However, in light of Boeing's announcement, Airbus had no other choice now than to aggressively explore this path. In an attempt to try to finally separate and differentiate from Boeing's shadow, Airbus announced that its mega plane would not be an extension of a current model but, instead, would be a brand new design. In March of 2000, Airbus introduced this new model with great fanfare. In an attempt to outdo Boeing, Airbus designed an aircraft that would be "double-decker," like the buses in London. Airbus got press around the world and many pundits started predicting the end of Boeing's supremacy and possibly the beginning of the end.

Exactly two weeks later, Boeing held its own press conference and no one expected to hear what they heard. Boeing announced to the world that, instead of imitating Airbus, Boeing was going to *reinvent the game*. The company told the world's press that it had decided to scrap its plans to extend the 747. Instead, it would build a new mid-size, *supersonic aircraft* that would reduce travel time by 40%, with the same operating costs as the jet-propelled airplane. All the experts agreed immediately. This was a much better strategy than Airbus's, since everyone knows that frequent fliers are not interested in traveling with *more people*, they simply want to get there *more quickly*.

Boeing has decided to change the game in an attempt to regain its supremacy. Now, for the key question: Do you really think that Boeing ever intended to build a "stretched" 747. My answer is: "Never in a million years!"

That announcement made back in 1999 was simply a ploy to entice Airbus into action and commit itself to a strategy that Boeing knew they could make obsolete very quickly. Airbus is now in the difficult position of having to retract its "mega plane" strategy and switch to a supersonic platform, about which they have very little knowledge, putting them 3 to 4 years behind Boeing.

One of the other concepts that we have been promoting for over twenty years is that a good strategy allows you to manage your competitor's business to your advantage as well as your own. This is achieved by attaining *supremacy of thinking* before you can attain *supremacy of strategy*.

Back To The Future

How does one go about changing, or even creating, a new game? The answer is simple: get out of the present and get into the future.

Chapter 3

Strategize
For The Future,
Not The Present

Formulating the business strategy of the enterprise is the top item on every CEO's job description. As a result, one would think that every company would have a clearly articulated and explicit strategy. Our work with over 400 corporations around the world has not proven that to be. In fact, we find that companies fall into one of four categories that revolve around two key capabilities–the organization's operational prowess and its strategic prowess. Strategic prowess is the kind of thinking that occurs in an organization that is *what* in nature. In other words, "*What* are we and *what* do we want to become?" Operational prowess is the kind of thinking that occurs in an organization that is *how* in nature or, "*How* do we get there?"

An element that adds to the difficulty of understanding the strategy of the business is that most people cannot distinguish between *strategy* and *operations*. Many have difficulty separating *strategy* and *strategic thinking* from *operations* and *operational thinking*. Although both types of thinking go on simultaneously in every organization, we have observed that these are practiced to different degrees of proficiency.

The difference can be explained by the following illustration.

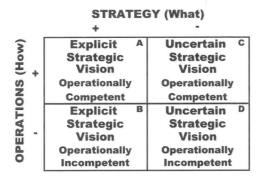

In quadrant A, we find companies that have a well articulated strategy, well communicated and well understood by everyone in the organization. They know *what* they want to become. Furthermore, they are very competent operationally. They know *how* to get there.

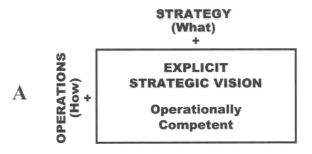

Examples of such companies are IBM and Lou Gerstner's formulation and deployment of his "co-centric computing" strategy. Other companies with clear strategies are Disney under Michael Eisner, Dell Computer under Michael Dell, Wal-Mart under Sam Walton and David Glass, and Home Depot under Bernie Marcus and Arthur Blank.

In quadrant B, we find companies that are operationally effective but strategically deficient. Many of the companies pursuing a me-too strategy fall into this quadrant.

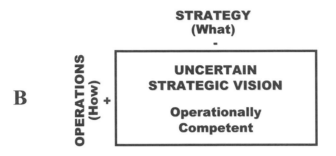

In quadrant C, we find companies that have a clear strategy. Their difficulty is making it happen operationally. A good example recently has been the PC industry with its 130 to 140 competitors all trying to be the best "Wintel" clone they can be. Clear strategy, but unfortunately, most of them have been unable to execute well operationally and the winners and losers change almost every day.

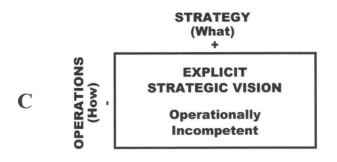

In quadrant D we find the worst of both worlds. Unfortunately, the list of examples is not very long because if you find yourself in this quadrant, you are not around long enough to talk about it.

In which quadrant do you think most companies find themselves? We have asked this question to more than 3000 CEOs all over the world and the answer is always the same. Eighty to ninety percent of these CEOs tell us that most companies reside in quadrant B: operationally competent but strategically deficient. Many CEOs even include their own company in this observation. In other words, most executives can keep the "numbers" coming out right quarter after quarter, but they don't have a shared understanding of what the company will look like as a result of all that churning. We call this the "Christopher Columbus School of Management":

- When he left, he did not know where he was going;
- When he got there, he did not know where he was;
- When he got back, he could not tell where he had been.

A good strategy should work to the benefit of an organization over a long period of time which implies that most companies should be in the "A" quadrant (+/+). Our experience has shown that most companies are actually in quadrant "B", begging the question: "Why?" Our answer to this question is that most executives are so mired in operational issues that they seldom have time to do any "strategizing." They spend all their time fighting fires and don't have time to think strategically. The best strategists are those that can foresee potential disruptive threats and turn these into a successful strategy that changes the game itself.

Key Skills

The creation of a "disruptive" strategy that will breed supremacy requires the mastery of two skills:

- Anticipation of future trends and their implications on society as well as on the organization

- Understanding of the organization's strategic capabilities that can be leveraged into these future trends

More and more CEOs that we work with tell us that it is not possible to predict the future because changes are occurring faster and faster. As a result, they claim, no one can keep up–much less predict what else will happen in the future.

Although this claim is partly true, the notion that change happens too quickly to be anticipated is somewhat of a myth. Our experience leads us to a different hypothesis. In our view, there are two modes to deal with changes: proactively or reactively. Most executives deal with most changes in a reactive mode. Their skill is *corrective* in nature rather than being proactive, or *anticipatory.* Proof of this is in the pudding. If their key skill were anticipatory, why were the CEOs and senior executives of thousands of corporations around the world caught by surprise by the advent of the Internet?

Envision The Future

"How can anyone anticipate what the future will look like? The future is a *big* place, and no one has a crystal ball." This is usually the statement we hear immediately after we offer the above hypothesis. The *arena* in which a company will compete in the future is not one with a limitless number of variables.

In fact, this reaction has a very simple and rational explanation. It has been shown that many things that look big and complex at first sight turn out to be an assembly of a limited number of smaller elements when scrutinized more closely. Thus it is with the future arena in which a company will compete. The future business arena in which any company will find itself consists of 12 discrete compartments from which disruptive trends might emerge:

- Economic/Monetary trends
- Political/Regulatory trends
- Social/Demographic trends
- Market conditions
- Customer attributes/habits
- Competitor profiles
- Next generation technology
- Manufacturing capabilities/processes
- Product design/content/features
- Sales/Marketing methods
- Distribution, delivery and service methods
- Human/natural/financial resources

Once the complexity of the future business arena has been deciphered into these 12 "building blocks," one can begin to anticipate what the future will look like. By placing yourself, and your key executives, in a "time machine" and moving yourself ahead "x" years and describing the characteristics that each compartment will have at that time, you will have a very good "picture" of the future.

Then comes the next objection: "We don't have any futurists in our company. How can we foresee changes that will occur in the future? No one has a crystal ball." The good news is that you don't need a guru to predict the future. Our contention is that most changes that will impact your business 10 years from now are in place today. *Most changes that will affect a company announce themselves well in advance of the time they will strike.*

As John Naisbitt, the renowned futurist, has said: "The best way to predict the future is to understand the present." In other words, the future has "folded" itself into the present, and one must "unfold" it to discover what is on the horizon. You must "go back" to the present to "see the future." But of course, if you have not been looking, you will always have a reactive, me-too strategy that will not bring supremacy.

Charles Schwab: Strategist "par excellence"

Some individuals have such an innate understanding of the concept of attaining strategic supremacy by changing the game rather than just the rules, that they have done it several times. Charles Schwab is such an individual. Schwab has an uncanny ability to anticipate future trends before his competitors do, and then create a new game.

Schwab founded Charles Schwab & Company in the 1970's by first changing the rules of the stock brokerage business, starting with the most cherished rule in the industry. He set transaction fees at half the industry norm. Furthermore, unlike his competitors, Schwab offered no research, one of the mostly costly services a broker extends. With these rule changes, Schwab spawned the discount brokerage business. Unfortunately, many imitators sprung up.

In 1995, however, Schwab decided to change the game itself. Schwab saw the growing dissatisfaction with ever increasing, and sometimes exorbitant, management fees that mutual funds imposed on their investors. The company introduced a program named One Source, which permitted investors to purchase a mix of mutual funds from a single source–Charles Schwab, naturally–rather than do so from each mutual fund company individually. The One Source program allowed each investor to choose from a portfolio of over 700 funds without paying any commission whatsoever and to switch from one fund to another without any penalty charge. The concept completely revolutionized the marketing of mutual funds and found the industry leader, Fidelity, asleep at the switch.

In 1997, Schwab decided to create yet another game. He introduced a program that allowed investors to trade stocks on-line. Within a matter of weeks, Schwab was trading over $4 billion per week which represented over 50% of its revenues. It has since climbed to over 90% of its revenues. This time, Schwab caught Merrill Lynch asleep at the switch. Until

Schwab introduced this program, stocks were traded over the phone through an army of highly paid sales people backed by expensive research. This new game has put that model in jeopardy and has forced all the brokerage houses to rethink their strategies and explore how they might respond. Unfortunately for them, the existing rule of selling through highly paid salespeople makes it extremely difficult to change but, more importantly, they would be playing on Schwab's game board and according to Schwab's rules.

Still not satisfied, Schwab has decided to change the game yet again. In June 2000, the company announced the purchase of U.S. Trust Corp., a money manager and financial adviser to the carriage trade where customers are not considered customers until they have been so for generations, not days, weeks or months. What the heck is Schwab doing in such an environment? Charles Schwab, being a very astute strategist, has glanced into the future and detected that there is a significant shift happening in the demographics of this country. It is a fact that sometime between the years 2010 and 2015, 50% of the U.S. population will be over 55 years old. Many of them will have inherited large sums of money and will now be faced with complex issues in an attempt to manage this wealth and preserve it for their children. Over 13 trillion dollars will be transferred from one generation to the next during this period. Many of the recipients of this wealth are probably current Schwab customers. Most will require personalized advice to help them optimize their returns. Do you get the connection? Is Charles Schwab about to create another new game? Stay tuned.

Insurance By The Minute

From a zero-based start in the 1970s, Progressive Insurance has become the nation's fourth largest auto insurer with revenues of over $6 billion. It did so initially by changing the rules of play.

In the car insurance industry, there is "golden" rule. "Don't insure drivers who have had an accident." That is an industry rule that no insurance company would ever violate. That is, until Progressive entered the game and changed the rules. Progressive did the exact opposite and *only* insured individuals who had had accidents…and at a premium nonetheless.

Until Progressive came along, all insurers calculated their risk exposure with a particular driver based on that driver's age and an accident-free past. In other words, only insure those individuals who have not had an accident. As a result, one can calculate the probability of risk quite accurately. The difficulty with this approach is that every other insurer is doing the same and everybody ends up with a "me-too" strategy that might match, but never gain supremacy over, those competitors.

Progressive's strategy was designed to do the exact opposite. Somewhere along the way, Progressive noticed that people who have had one accident rarely have any more. Progressive's mathematicians got to work and confirmed that the probability of someone having a second accident was *lower* than that of having their first. Thus, the growth of Progressive to this day.

Now, Progressive is about to change the game itself. Anticipating a future where most people will be at ease with all the gadgets of the digital age, Progressive is conducting a pilot program in Texas that could revolutionize the auto insurance industry and make Progressive the focal point of that new game. The company has installed in several cars, devices that measure the amount of time that the car is in use, who is driving and, through a link-up to a Global Positioning Satellite (GPS), where the car went. All this data is captured on-line and transmitted back to Progressive which then uses it to calculate that driver's premium. In other words, *insurance by the minute!* Like a meter in a parking lot, you only pay for the time used. Sounds like Progressive may have another home run on its hands.

Disrupting The Future

The CEOs of these two companies obviously are excellent strategists and have an uncanny ability to disrupt their competitors' future over and over again. Which makes one wonder why so many executives are unable to foresee trends or events that might seriously disrupt a healthy strategy and put it in jeopardy overnight. This usually happens because these executives fail to foresee the advent of a totally different kind of disruptor, one we call the *stealth disruptor.*

Chapter 4

The
Stealth Disruptors:
A CEO's Worst Nightmare

A few years ago, the CEOs of the two dominant book retailers in the United States–Barnes & Noble and Borders–were sitting in their respective offices, listening to the business news on CNN's *Moneyline*, contemplating ways and means of taking away some of each other's business.

During the newscast, there was a short interview with a gentleman named Jeff Bezos, who declared that he had formed a company named *amazon.com* which, effective immediately, would start selling books on-line through the Internet. Furthermore, he stated that amazon.com would carry over 1,000,000 titles, a hundred times the average bookstore; that the price would be 30-50% less than in a bookstore; and that a purchase could be made in a couple of minutes from the comfort of one's home by simply using a PC

A few weeks later, the CEO of Merrill Lynch was thinking about ways and means to compete with Smith Barney while watching the same TV program. Another young entrepreneur announced the launch of an on-line brokerage company called *E-Trade.com* which would allow individuals to trade stocks from their home PCs at a fraction of the cost of going through a broker.

Only days later, another Internet entrepreneur announced the start of a company called *priceline.com* which would allow an individual to purchase airline tickets on-line at a price that individual wanted to pay and not at the exorbitant price that the airlines would want that individual to pay.

Ama...who? E...who? Price...who? Doing...what? must have been the reaction of these CEOs on the day of these announcements. All were caught completely off-guard by this announcement and since then, these new companies have become each CEO's biggest nightmare.

The day that amazon.com went on-line, Barnes & Nobles' and Borders' business models were put into jeopardy. The day that E-Trade.com went on-line, Merrill Lynch's business model of selling stocks through thousands of highly commissioned salespeople was put into jeopardy. The day that autobytel.com went on-line, Wayne Huizenga's Autonation business model of selling cars by offering thousands of models displayed on massive car lots was put into jeopardy. The day that Jay Walker went on-line with priceline.com, the entire airline industry's business model was put into jeopardy.

The situations described above, as well as many others which have since occurred, bring two intriguing questions:

- Why is it that the business models of dominant enterprises, led by astute CEOs, can be put into jeopardy overnight?

- What can be done to mitigate, or even reverse, the impact?

Well-established, dominant enterprises, or even an entire industry, can be "killed" or seriously injured by the advent of a so-called "stealth" competitor which had not been on the CEO's "radar screen."

Enter The Stealth Competitor

Why was NCR (National Cash Register) caught totally by surprise and not able to foresee the advent of microprocessors as replacements for their electromechanical cash registers? After all, NCR was the dominant player in that game and had the resources to employ hundreds of futurists who could have done just that.

Why was Singer, which had invented the sewing machine, and had put one in just about every home in the developed world, caught in the same trap? Why was IBM, the powerhouse of the computer industry, also taken by surprise by Apple's introduction of the Macintosh PC?

Why were RCA and Zenith also caught completely off-guard by Sony's introduction of the VCR and the Walkman? After all, they were the largest, strongest and richest in their industry and should have foreseen Sony's entrance into their sandbox?

Stuck In The Current Sandbox

In our view, a major contributor to the inability of executives to anticipate the advent of stealth competitors that may put them out of business, is that they are stuck in the *current* sandbox. In other words, their time is consumed with their preoccupation with *current* products, for *current* customers, in *current* market segments residing in *current* geographic markets. Although this is a necessary element of management, a more vital responsibility of management is to be more concerned about the company's *future* products, *future* customers, *future* markets and *future* competitors. This should, in particular, include the stealth competitor that may come from another sandbox or from any of the sources we will now explore.

Supremacy of the game board, or sandbox, will only occur if the strategy is designed *for the future, not the present.* The most successful CEOs, in our view, spend most their time anticipating the *future.* They have mastered the ability to anticipate the sources that disruptive stealth competitors could emerge from and have developed strategies to be the disruptor to their competitors instead.

Disruptive Changes And Stealth Competitors

There are five broad areas from which a stealth competitor can emerge and become your worst nightmare.

■ Political/Regulatory Environment

These are radical changes that occur in either the political or the regulatory arenas. Some political examples are the fall of the Berlin Wall or the opening of China. These two changes will have an enormous impact on the future of businesses worldwide as they will bring another 2 billion people into a "free market" economy. On the other hand, they will also bring several hundred new competitors.

■ Demographics

Changes in demographics are another source that can disrupt many industries simultaneously. There are four types of demographics that can cause this:

> * income distribution
> * age distribution
> * education levels
> * population shifts/mixes

An example is the aging of the population in Japan, the United States and Europe, and the opposite trend in places such as Mexico and Asia. This dichotomy will disrupt the strategies of many corporations. Oil companies, for instance, should be re-thinking their concept of the self-service gas station since older people are not as mobile and cannot serve themselves as easily as younger ones.

■ Industry/Market Structural Changes

Radical changes in the structure of an industry or market will always bring disruption to many companies. In this category one needs to monitor such elements as deregulation which caused havoc in the airline industry in the 1980's; or privatization such as is happening to many state owned telecom and postal service organizations in several countries; or consolidation as is currently happening in the oil, drug and several other industries; or rationalization of industries. Each of these events will disrupt the strategies of many companies simultaneously.

■ Perception

This is one of the most difficult to detect, but it can disrupt companies in a major manner. It is the change in perception that customers have about a company's product. The ways in which customers perceive products are not static. Their perception of the look, feel or benefits of the products they buy changes with time. An example is the cigarette. In the 50's and 60's smoking was "cool." In the 80's and 90's, it was "uncool." That change in perception will eventually bring that entire industry to its knees.

■ Technology

Technological advances, obviously, can also bring disruption to many industries. Two kinds of technological advances can have this type of impact. One consists, naturally, of breakthroughs such as the laser, the microprocessor, the Internet and the science of biotechnology.

Another is the convergence, or fusion, of different technologies such as the marriage of computer and telecommunication technologies or the coupling of computers and biotechnology.

Changes Come In Three Sizes

Changes that may emanate from any of the above sources come in three sizes–micro, macro and mega.

Micro changes are those that happen every day at ground level. They are relatively easy to detect and we take care of these routinely and then go on with our lives. Micro changes have a limited effect. They will affect a very limited number of products, customers or markets. An example might be the deregulation of the Italian Post Office. Although an important event in Italy, the effects of that change will probably be limited to Italy's borders.

Macro changes affect a much broader array of products, customers or markets. They are "once in a generation" types of changes and can only be detected from around 20,000 feet above the Earth. Macro changes are not as easily detected as micro ones. Failure to detect a macro change could be fatal to a company. Two such changes are at work today and many CEOs have not noticed. One is the dichotomy in the age demographics of the "western" world versus Mexico and Asia as mentioned above. This dichotomy will cause every company that does, or intends to do, business in these areas of the world, to rethink their product designs.

If you are a manufacturer of exercise equipment, for example, the older people of the "western" world will need radically different exercise machines than the young turks in these other countries.

If you want to achieve supremacy in your field, you will need a strategy that can accommodate this dichotomy or else a stealth competitor might just be around the corner.

Mega changes are "once in a century" type of changes. They can usually be detected in their embryonic stage. But they are different enough in character that many executives don't quite understand them, and therefore, cannot assess the implications of these on their businesses. This can also be fatal since mega changes affect *every product, every customer, every market, every company, every industry, in every country on the planet.* They will also affect the "genetic code" of every enterprise and usually are the source of dozens of "stealth" competitors. This is so because their disruption is usually brought on by the advent of radical new technology. Two such technologies are currently giving CEOs fits. One is the Internet, whose impact is already being felt by many corporations. The other is biotechnology, whose impact is yet to come but will be even more pronounced than the Internet.

Stealth competitors accompany these mega changes because it is usually people who understand these new technologies that use it first. Witness to this phenomenon is the advent of all the "dot coms" during the 90's that were started by young people who understood the capabilities of the Internet and how to use these capabilities against well established, but totally unprepared, companies.

Lurking In The Shadows

The cozy world of university Presidents, Deans and Professors is about to be dismantled in the next 10 to 15 years. The game in this industry is well known to all the players and has been in place for several hundred years. These rules are simple to understand:

- choose a charming geographic location
- build a lot of buildings, each to accommodate a different discipline
- give these buildings a distinctive architectural look and feel
- hire "name" professors that will put the university "on the map"
- promise these professors "tenure," or lifetime employment if they enhance their reputations by getting their works published
- seek wealthy alumni to contribute to your endowment
- start an MBA summer school to attract high level executives to solidify your relationships with industry

That formula has worked successfully for many universities for several centuries. Lurking in the shadows is a stealth competitor that is not on most traditional universities' "radar screens." This new entrant is called the University of Phoenix. Unlike the traditional universities, the U of P does not have a campus in a charming little town. In fact, it has no campus at all. Nor does it have any buildings–no bricks and mortar.

Therefore, no classrooms. And even more interesting–there are no students and no professors on site. What the University of Phoenix does have, however, is the Internet…and 90,000 students, very few of whom are in Phoenix. It also is a public shareholder company with a market cap of over $2.8 billion. The U of P's forecast calls for an enrollment of over 100,000 on-line students and annual revenues of $1billion in the next three years.

John Sperling, the university's founder and a former history professor, has not only changed the rules but has changed the game of higher education itself.

FedEx Disrupts Another Sandbox

If priceline.com and Southwest weren't enough to give fits to the CEOs of American, United and Delta, a new "stealth" competitor is about to enter their sandbox and cause a major disruption. FedEx, which has perfected the delivery of letters and parcels, recently announced that it will shortly enter the "shipping" of people. And it will do this by changing the game of travel.

Instead of offering coach, business or first class seats at exorbitant fares, FedEx will put you in a "people pak" which will consist of a 7' x 3' envelope with a 10" foam cushion. These will accommodate an adult weighing up to 230 lbs. Somewhat like an oversized sleeping bag, these human "envelopes" will have a rigid fiberglass skeleton that will allow it to be stacked in racks that will take up to four passengers.

Travel will be, as with packages, overnight. The fares will be calculated on the distance traveled and will average around $89 each way. This new disruptor, which I am certain none of the major airlines had on their radar screens, is bound to appeal to a large segment of the population and take considerable share of market. Even Southwest should be concerned about this new entrant.

Strategy Test

Is your strategy ready for an unforeseen, unexpected stealth competitor that could become your worst nightmare? Or will you be the one to anticipate what strategy a "stealth competitor" might conceive to establish supremacy in your sandbox? In the past year, several of our clients have used our process to do just that and have embraced the stealth strategy for themselves, or have found ways to neutralize it. The next chapter describes some examples.

Chapter 5

Supremacy Models
From Client Organizations

For the last year we have been using our Strategic Supremacy Process that we started developing a few years ago with a number of clients. This has allowed us to validate our concepts and prove that they work in the "real world." Only *after* the concepts and the process had been validated did we write this book.

One part of our process calls for the formation of a "stealth" competitor team whose mandate is to develop a "stealth" strategy and business model that would result in supremacy over all competitors in the sandbox of the future. The full mandate that this team is given is:

- that the "stealth" competitor needs to be an organization that is not currently on our "radar screen" but will be interested in the Business Arena we will be part of in the future
- that the intent is nothing less than supremacy of the sandbox
- that the strategy and business model must be one that can actually be deployed by some company if not your own

The following are examples from five of our clients. Each of these "stealth" strategies represents a dramatic departure from their current strategy. They also are strategies that will allow these companies to break "out of the box," rid themselves of "me-too" strategies, *differentiate* themselves from their competitors and substantially increase the probability of asserting supremacy in their respective sandboxes.

The HVAC.com Strategy

There is a market out there known as the HVAC market. HVAC stands for "heating, ventilation and air conditioning." In this market, or sandbox, there are a number of companies that supply equipment and products such as boilers, furnaces, air conditioners, floorboard heating panels, ceiling ducts, etc, etc, etc.

There are approximately two dozen players in the sandbox, one of which is our client which offers a wide variety of such products. The game, in this sandbox, is currently played according to the following rules:

- Most manufacturers work through Reps
- Most manufacturers have a love/hate relationship with their Reps
- All manufacturers interact with a number of parties such as developers, contractors, builders, and architects, and there are a number of contacts with each before obtaining an order
- All attempt to get "spec'd in" the customer's blueprint which guarantees a long relationship with that customer
- All work on the same price structure with the same volume and trade discounts
- All work through third party installers
- All manufacturers have very little name recognition with the end user and, frequently, even within the industry
- The industry is highly fragmented

During the Strategic Supremacy sessions with us, a "stealth" team was formed and given the mandate to develop a strategy that would reign supreme in the sandbox of the future. Looking at the Future Business Arena, which the group had developed that morning, they decided that one of the major impediments to the conduct of business in this sandbox is that there are too many parties with which a manufacturer needs to interact. All these contacts slow the flow and often negatively affect the accuracy of the information needed to consummate a transaction. The team felt that a company that could reduce the number of players and streamline the information flow would achieve supremacy in the future sandbox.

The concept? HVAC.com. This company would be the hub for all players in the sandbox and the game would be changed in the following manner:

- HVAC.com would join the best manufacturers of different equipment into a network of "premier" suppliers to the HVAC sandbox.

- On the other side, this new entity would attempt to have the buyers–contractors, architects, developers–join a "private" club for customers of HVAC products.

- As a premier manufacturer, you would receive "privileged" information from HVAC.com, which would keep you abreast of what's going on in the sandbox. This would include information about upcoming construction projects, the names of the developer and contractor, and the mechanics of the bid process (who the competitors are likely to be, etc.).

- As a member of the private customer club, you would also receive "privileged" information such as advanced notice on new products, changes in standards and codes, and group discounts if you purchased all of your products from HVAC.com members.

How would all this happen and how would the flow of information be streamlined? The answer: the Internet. Here are the two models:

Current Model

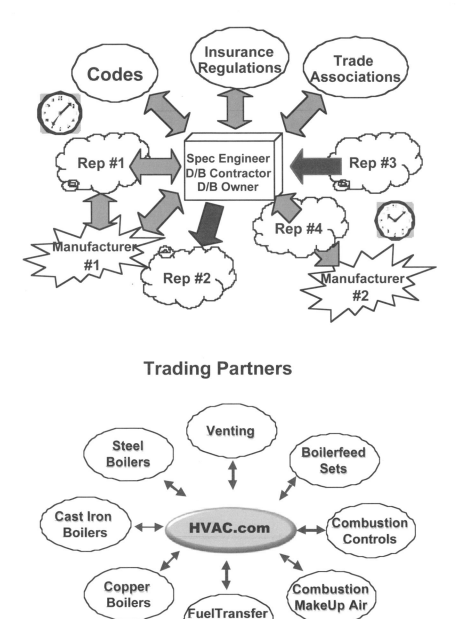

Trading Partners

New Model

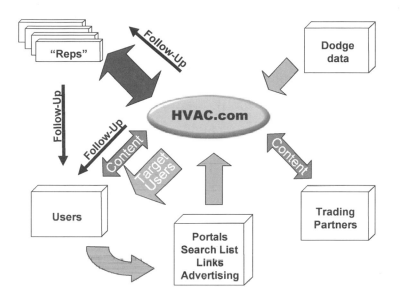

Food Retailing As It Will Be

Food retailing has probably been around since man has been on this planet and the game has not changed much over that period of time. It started with farmers bringing their produce to the open markets in nearby cities and displaying their produce on stands the best way they could in order to attract as many customers as possible. About the only major change that has occurred over the centuries is that these markets are now indoors, instead of outdoors. In today's indoor supermarket sandbox, the game is played in this manner:

- Build a store with 50,000 to 75,000 square feet of space
- Locate these stores in densely populated areas in metropolitan cities and suburbs
- Install row upon row of display shelves separated by aisles that you expect the customers to follow, all going in the same direction at the same time

- Stock the shelves with large quantities of perishable and non-perishable goods which you hope will be purchased rapidly since the cost of keeping these in inventory is very high
- Build end-of-aisle merchandising displays with discounted prices good only for a limited time
- Use coupons and other promotional techniques to attract potential customers
- Build a "chain" of these stores to develop brand name recognition and benefit from economies of scale

Every retailer, including our client, operates this way and no one has supremacy. In fact the CEO of this company opened the work session with the following introduction:

"Although we are operationally competent and as a result have been reasonably successful over the years, our position in the marketplace has not changed in the last 32 years. The reason is that all the competitors in our sandbox are cloning each other and no one gains at the others' expense. In the last few years, we've come to realize that we must have a distinctive strategy that will set us apart from these competitors so that we can enhance our market position.

"Since then, we have been searching for assistance but had not found anything satisfactory until we encountered DPI. Their process of Strategic Thinking and the concept of a "stealth" competitor intrigued us and thus the reason why we are here today. We must change our strategy and do something different or else our future will be no better than our past and that is not acceptable.

"Our strategy is equal to that of our competitors and we must find a strategy that will place us well above these competitors if we want to outpace them in the marketplace."

A stealth team was formed which developed a very different strategy that has a much higher probability of achieving supremacy. The strategy which they developed is based on the following observations that they foresaw about the Future Business Arena.

- Since people will be under more and more time pressure, they will have less time to shop. Therefore, a supremacy strategy should give customers the possibility to shop by whatever method is convenient to them. This would include shopping in person, by phone, fax or over the Internet.
- Although most people are willing to buy packaged goods sight unseen, they usually want to "see and feel" fresh goods such as meat, fish, fruit and vegetables.
- Some people are quite willing to come to the store to get their food, but more and more people have less and less time to do so
- Going through cashiers is also time consuming and unproductive. A quicker method of paying for groceries would be welcomed
- Shopping twice a week, too, is a pain and reducing this frequency would be an added benefit

With these observations in hand, the team then created a new game that a potential "stealth" entrant would use to attain supremacy in the food-retailing sandbox. The new game will have a dramatically different set of rules:

- Stores will no longer be fifty to seventy-five thousand square feet but rather in the range of 25,000 to 30,000 square feet
- Stores will no longer be rectangular in shape but circular
- Traffic will be in one direction, moving around a circle instead of moving up and down aisles, often in opposite directions
- Non-perishable items will be displayed, with only one sample on display, on shelves arranged inside the circle
- Fresh goods will be displayed in separate "cavities" built on the perimeter of the outside wall
- These areas will be staffed by an "expert" in each domain, such as a butcher at the meat counter, and the same at the fish, produce and fruit counters
- In fact, the entire store's décor will have a "theme" to give it a distinctive "look and feel" to make shopping an "experience" rather than a task
- There will be a number of smaller, "satellite" stores located strategically around each neighborhood, replenished by the hub store on a daily basis

- Customers will be able to shop in a number of ways:
  + at the "hub" store
  + by phone, fax or the Internet
  + pick-up can be at the hub stores or
  one of the satellite stores
  + the non-perishable products could be
  delivered automatically once a month,
  and one goes to the store for the fresh
  goods when needed
- A plastic card will also track your purchases and warn you when you might need refills

How will all this be paid for? A self-service scanner attached to every shelf reads the bar code on the product and keeps a running count of your purchases, thus eliminating the need to wait in line at the cash counter.

Our CEO-client was so impressed by this strategy that he decided to embrace it and immediately authorized a pilot store be built to test the concept. If it proves successful, the strategy will be deployed in all corners of their sandbox in the next few years. Be on the lookout for this new store in your neighborhood soon.

One-Step Real Estate Transactions

If you've ever bought real estate, you are aware of the multitude of tasks necessary to complete the transaction. Another one of our clients is in the midst of changing that game in a dramatic manner. That client has been, until now, a title insurance company. Every real estate transaction requires that the "title" of the property, in other words, ownership, be free and clear of liens. Thus, the moniker "title insurance company." Today, the game is played this way:

- The Real Estate agent contacts the Title Insurance company and asks for a "search" of the "title"
- The Title Insurance company goes to municipal archives and does a manual search of past transactions to ascertain that there are no encumbrances on the property in question

- The Real Estate agent then has to coordinate a number of other activities before the sale can be consummated
- These include:
  * arranging for an inspection of the property to insure that the property is in good shape and that there are no structural flaws
  * arranging for the financing of the property through a bank or mortgage lender
  * arranging for a lawyer, or notary, to prepare all the documents that need to be signed

Plus a dozen, or more, such tasks. Our client is about to change that game radically. Using our process, this company formulated a new strategy which will make it, over time, the focal point of every real estate transaction in the country. The ultimate goal of this new strategy is to be the *"transaction manager"* of all real estate transfers that happen in the United States. In the very near future, Real Estate agents will be able to go to one source, our client, to obtain all these services. Furthermore, when a seller will decide to put up a property for sale, he/she will be able to have many of these services performed in *advance*, thus accelerating the consummation of the transaction. An example would be the inspection which the "transaction manager" would have done before any buyer is found. Our client would then give that buyer a "Good Housekeeping Seal of Approval" that the property is in acceptable condition. A visual illustration of this new strategy is shown below.

Closing Room & Transaction Manager

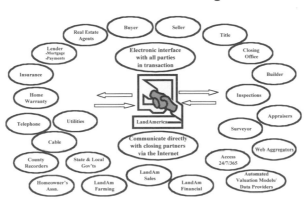

Images "Anywhere, Anytime"

Since Sony announced, in 1984, the development of a "digital" camera, the photographic world has not been the same. That announcement sent tremors throughout the industry and was a wake-up call for companies such as Kodak and Polaroid. In fact, Kodak is still feeling the aftershocks. So it was for our client as well since they are manufacturers of equipment that converts "negatives" into "hard copy" photo images. "Digital" images displayed on screens, instead of hard copy, are a death threat to such a company. This client, therefore, had been scrambling for several years looking for another strategy. Wisely, it had made a few acquisitions of a number of small companies which were dabbling in this new digital world. Unfortunately, all these entities were operating in their own separate worlds with little, if any, contact with each other. All that changed when they assembled to go through our process.

During that process, they came to similar conclusions as to what the Future Business Arena would be. The main conclusion was that, in the future, people will probably want to see their images in both digital and analog (hard copy) formats. In other words, there will still be life for analog imaging equipment. The next realization was that they were the only company that had expertise in *both* sandboxes. Furthermore, they concluded that the game in the future will be played very differently than it is today and that their future competition will not come from their current competitors but rather from a group of "stealth" companies that were not on their radar screens.

Their view of the Future Business Arena is that images will be captured with either analog or digital devices, transmitted somewhere else, and displayed in either analog or digital formats, or both. At the capture and at the display extremities, the competitors would no longer be Kodak or Fuji but rather Sony, Hewlett Packard, Epson, Canon, Sharp and several others. The transmission stage, which will occur over the Internet or over telephone lines and even through cable, would attract yet another class of competitors. These would consist of the telecoms of the world and others such as AOL Time Warner as well as the cable TV operators. All to say, a dramatically different sandbox.

Our client's new strategy? Achieve supremacy in this sandbox by developing equipment that can ease the capture and display of images in either analog *or* digital formats. An example is a new product that they conceived from their use of the "stealth" concept.

Let's assume that you, like many others, have taken a large number of pictures with your digital camera and you would like to send a hard copy of some of these images to another party. Today, that is very difficult to do. One project that our client will develop will work as follows. They will develop a product that will look like, but be smaller than, an ATM machine. You will be able to take your images, put them on a floppy diskette or on a CD, and insert it into their machine. The machine will then transmit your images to a similar one located close to your intended recipient and give those images to that person either in hard copy form or on a floppy or CD, whichever that person prefers.

Now take this concept to the next level. Imagine yourself at Disney World and you have taken pictures of your children all day in various entourages and you would like Grandma to see the enjoyment that your kids are experiencing. At the end of each day, you would simply make your way over to our client's kiosk, attach your camera to an input link and transmit your photos directly to Grandma's PC. Grandma could then view the pictures on her monitor or else print them using a printing device made by our client. Grandma would experience your children's enjoyment remotely, but instantly.

Images. Anywhere. Anytime.

Several Homes, Same Developer

Another of our clients is one of the largest developers of homes in the United States. To date, the residential property game is played in the following manner:

- Developers "specialize" in certain categories of home building such as stand alone housing, apartments, condos, custom-built, assisted living, and so forth

- Most developers build what they call "communities" which include parks, recreation centers, shopping centers, medical facilities, bike paths, walking trails, and so forth
- They also specialize by price category such as low-end, mid-range and high-end homes
- They are always searching out new parcels of land for future projects
- They control the design of these homes but contract out the actual building to outside firms
- Many operate in several geographic markets
- They build model homes as tantalizers to lure prospective buyers
- The industry is highly fragmented and no one competitor has more than 2% of the total market

This game is about to be changed dramatically. Our client, also using the stealth concept, determined that supremacy and a significantly much larger market share could be obtained by developing a strategy that would capitalize on an aspect of the business that is not considered today. That is the realization that at different stages of their lives, people want different types of homes. Therefore, a developer that could offer a spectrum of homes built to the changing needs of people would have a good chance of keeping these buyers during their entire life span, thus attaining supremacy in the home building sandbox.

This, generally, represents the evolution of a couple's housing needs over their lifetime:

- upon marriage, they usually want a "starter" home or an apartment, located close to where they work
- with the arrival of children, they now want a larger home with access to community services such as shopping centers, medical clinics, recreation parks, etc.
- if their careers take off, they may wish to move into a larger home in a more affluent part of town
- they may even be transferred to another city but would like to reside in a home similar to the one they currently have
- when the children grow up and leave for college, they now want to "downsize" into a home that requires less effort to maintain

- upon retirement, they may even move to Florida or some other location and live in a condo within a retirement community

That is the strategy that our client is in the process of deploying. The company will start building communities of homes to satisfy the evolving lifestyle needs of their customers. Their intent is to be the only developer that their customers buy homes from throughout their lives. Today, as customers move from one lifestyle to another, they also move from one developer to another, sometimes with unsatisfactory results. Our client concluded that if customers are satisfied with the first "starter" home which they purchase, there is a high probability that these customers would prefer buying their second, third and even fourth homes from the same developer instead of taking a risk on a new, unknown vendor.

The strategy: Once a customer, forever a customer.

Observations

After some two dozen experiences with the "stealth" competitor approach to the formulation of a future strategy for an enterprise, here are some observations we have made:

- every client to date has concluded that the Future Business Arena will be dramatically different than the current sandbox
- every client has concluded that the lines of demarcation between sandboxes are getting more and more blurred
- every client has identified new potential "stealth" competitors that could enter their sandbox and make life extremely difficult for them
- every client has concluded that the "stealth" scenarios developed during our process were realistic and that some organization would pursue such a strategy if they chose not to do so themselves
- every client ended up altering their current strategy dramatically to incorporate many, if not all, of the elements of the "stealth" strategy

How does one go about deciding whether or not adopting part or all of a stealth strategy makes sense? The answer to this question, in our view, is the mastery of the concepts and a process we call Strategic Thinking. Strategic Thinking is the only competitive advantage a CEO and the

Executive Team have over their competitors. To outthink their competitors, not to outmuscle them in the marketplace, is what leads to strategic supremacy. As General Eisenhower once said:

"Wars are won in the Planning Room, not on the battlefield."

Chapter 6

Strategic Thinking: The Essence of Competitive Supremacy

As noted earlier, the majority of CEOs we surveyed placed their companies in the Christopher Columbus School of Management–that is, in the quadrant characterized by operational competence but strategic uncertainty. Intrigued, we started looking into the barriers, obstacles, and impediments that prevent companies from operating in the upper left quadrant, the ideal one to be in. To identify the various obstacles, we went back to these companies to find out how they were run by their CEOs.

Obstacles To Strategic Thinking

We noticed very quickly that people who run companies spend a lot of their time in meetings of one kind or another. My friends at 3M, for example, tell me that when people are appointed "managers," they spend 80 to 90 percent of their time in meetings, talking and talking to one another! In many companies, these people have been meeting and talking for years.

The Strategy Suffers From "Fuzzy Vision"

It would seem logical, then, for people in management to have a shared and clear vision of what lay ahead for their organizations. However, when we asked them to describe what their company might look like in the future, we got very different pictures. Each person gave us a distinct version of **what** that "look" would be.

Obstacles To
Good Strategic Thinking

Strategies can suffer from fuzzy vision.

Management Is Engulfed In Operational Minutiae

That led us to our next question: "What do they talk about?" And what do
you think we heard them talking about during all those meetings? Right!
They talked about operational issues rather than strategic issues. This
means that the "look" of the organization starts being shaped by outside
forces.

OPERATIONAL

STRATEGIC

Operational minutiae block strategic thought.

And there are many outside forces that will gladly take over the strategy and direction of your company if you abdicate your right to do so yourself. These forces include your customers by the nature of demands they make on your organization–those that you respond to and those that you do not.

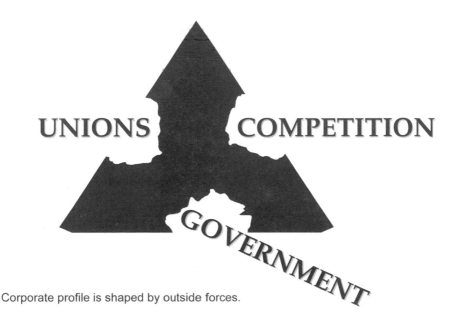

UNIONS   COMPETITION

GOVERNMENT

Corporate profile is shaped by outside forces.

No Crisis, No Strategy

We further observed that when times are good, and all the charts, graphs, and numbers are going through the roof, managers have things on their minds other than asking themselves: "Where is this business going?"

Good times put off strategic thinking.

Only in times of crisis, when resources become scarce and limited resources must be allocated more carefully, does the need to think strategically surface. Our view is that strategic thinking is an ongoing process during good times or bad times. In fact, if you wait until the bad times, it obviously becomes more difficult to do.

No Formal Process

The most important obstacle to sound strategic thinking that we discovered was the lack of a formal process.

Strategy depends on a formal process.

Periodically, we would come across a well-intentioned management team that said to itself: "Let's go up to the mountaintop for a weekend and discuss where this business is going." People would then make their way to the retreat, sit around a table, put their elbows up, and start looking at each other. After seven minutes of silence, one of them would finally ask: "Now that we're here, what do we do? Where do we start?" After another seven minutes of silence, guess what kinds of issues they were discussing again? Right! Operational issues–the very issues they didn't want to discuss in the first place.

Even well-led and well-managed companies–including such clients as Caterpillar, 3M, and Dow Corning–did not have a formal process to help them decide what they wanted to become in the future. This observation led DPI to concentrate its efforts and research on the answer to a simple question: "If there is a process to help a company determine its future, what is that process?" In other words, "What questions should people be asking themselves while they are sitting around this table, and in what order should they go through these questions?"

Therefore, when we work with a client, we bring the *questions* and we guide the management team through these questions in a structured and systematic manner. Again, however, it is their *input* going into the process and it is their *output* coming out of the process. This gives the management team complete and absolute ownership of the strategy. A strategy that has been created by the people who have a vital stake in the future of an organization gets implemented much more quickly and much more successfully than one that is imposed on the organization by an outside third party.

The Origins Of Strategic Thinking

The 1970s saw the advent of strategic planning as a key tool proposed by consultants to aid corporate managements in determining the future of their organizations. Most strategic planning systems, however, relied on historical data–numbers–that were generated internally. These systems required long and exhaustive analyses with a heavy numerical base. The result was an extrapolation of history into the future. The skill required: *quantitative analysis.*

Strategic thinking, on the other hand, incorporates an assessment of both the internal and external environments. The data are highly subjective and consist of the personal perceptions of each member of the management team. Most of the data are stored in each person's head. The key is to tap into that knowledge base and bring these perceptions into an objective forum for rational debate. The process involves a qualitative evaluation of the business and its environment and is both introspective and extrospective. The skill required: *qualitative synthesis.*

During the 1970s, when strategic planning was at its pinnacle, an avalanche of books appeared under a variety of titles: *Strategic Management, Corporate Strategy, Strategy THIS,* and *Strategy THAT.* Because of my experience in marketing positions at the time, I was attracted to many of these books and started browsing through them to gain a better understanding of strategy.

As I started going through these books, I made two very quick discoveries. First, every author who mentioned "strategy" assigned the word a different meaning. One author claimed that strategy was the *goal* and that operations was the *tactic*. The next author insisted that the "goal" definition was wrong. Rather, the goal was the *objective* and strategy was the *means*. The next author defined strategy as *long-term planning* and tactics as *short-term planning*. Needless to say, I became more and more confused as I read.

The second discovery I made was that all these books were written by academics who ensconced themselves in business school libraries before posing the question of the century: "What has made General Electric so successful?" And without ever speaking to anyone at GE, but strictly by observing organizations from the outside, they concocted the "miracle" recipes that these so-called winning organizations had used and then published books extolling their "findings."

We at DPI decided to do our research in a very different manner. We said to ourselves: "Let's go and talk to *real* people who run *real* organizations and ask them how they go about deciding the future of their companies." And we did just that. We started interviewing CEOs in a variety of different-size companies in a variety of different industries in dozens of countries. Eventually, we even sat in on meetings which CEOs had with their management teams while they were talking "strategy." Therefore, the concepts described in the remainder of this book are not "miracle" recipes pulled out of the sky. Rather, they represent a process that was extracted from the heads of real CEOs running real companies.

Strategic Supremacy: Taking Strategic Thinking To The Next Level

The Strategic Supremacy concepts we are describing in this book have their roots in our original process of Strategic Thinking. However, they take our original concepts to a higher level with the addition of new concepts such as the Future Business Area, the advent of "stealth" competitors and the development of a Supremacy Model. Even our new process of Strategic Supremacy, though, starts with the CEO's vision for the future of the organization.

The CEO's Vision: The Cornerstone Of Strategy

As we started talking to CEOs, we noticed that within minutes of the start of such a discussion, they would start speaking of a certain "vision" they had for the future of their company.

The CEO's Vision.

Frequently what a CEO envisioned his or her company to "look like" in the future was somewhat different from what it "looks like" today.

A new "look" for the future.

What Is Strategic Thinking?

Creating a vision is akin to painting a picture. Warren Buffett, the renowned investor and founder of Berkshire describes it this way: "Berkshire is my painting, so it should look the way I want it to look."

In complete agreement with the above, we came to describe strategic *thinking*, as opposed to strategic planning, as the kind of thinking that goes on in the heads of the CEO and the management team as they attempt to transform their vision into a *profile*, or *picture*, of what the company will "look like" at some point in the future.

The strategic profile actualizes the vision.

They then would "hang" that profile, or picture, up as a target for all their plans and decisions. Decisions that fit inside the "frame" of the profile were pursued, while those that did not were abandoned. In other words, that profile, or picture, became the "filter" for all their plans and decisions.

Target for all plans.

Why would a CEO want to design a profile for the future of the company? The answer is simple: to ensure that people make consistent and intelligent decisions on behalf of the company. Which leads to the next question: "If I want my people to make good decisions on my behalf, what do I paint inside that picture to help them do that?" or, "How does the profile of a company transform itself into tangible or physical elements?" Or still, "What elements of a company could I touch or feel that would be tangible evidence of its strategy and direction?"

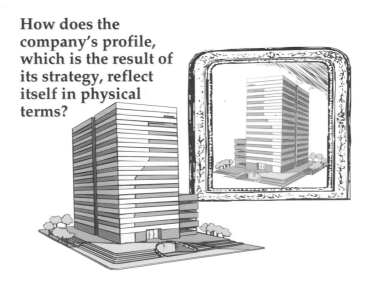

How does the company's profile, which is the result of its strategy, reflect itself in physical terms?

Input And Outputs

To this question, there are several answers. I could look at the company's portfolio of current and announced products. That would be one "clue." I could look at its facilities to see what they produced and where they were located. That would be another clue. I could look at its base of customers and where they reside–its geographic markets. I could examine its competitors and its suppliers. These are other clues. Gradually, as I look at each "piece" of the company, the "puzzle" starts taking shape in my mind as to what that organization will "look like" in the future.

- Products
- Facilities
- Technology
- Talent
- Customers
- Suppliers
- Industry segments
- Distribution methods
- Geographic markets
- Production capabilities
- Competitors
- Selling methods

The "look," or profile of a company that is the "result" of its strategy resides in four of the areas listed above. Specifically the profile of a company finds itself in the nature of

- The products that the company decides to offer
- The customers to whom it offers these products
- The industry segments that it decides to pursue
- The geographic markets that it seeks

All the other elements listed above are either *inputs* to this profile or *outputs* from this profile.

PROFILE

Key content areas of the strategic profile.

In order for a CEO to give *clear* direction, however, the strategic profile needs to be taken a step further and embrace the following content:

- It needs to identify the nature of products that will be offered but, more importantly, the nature of products that will *not* be offered.

- It needs to identify the types of customers to concentrate on but, more importantly, the types of customers *not* to concentrate on.

- It needs to identify the industry segments to pursue but, more importantly, the industry segments *not* to pursue.

- It needs to identify the geographic markets to be sought but, more importantly, the geographic markets *not* to be sought.

STRATEGIC PROFILE

Strategic content includes areas of greater and lesser emphasis.

The Strategic Profile Becomes A Filter For Decision Making

Why should a CEO's vision be transformed into a strategic profile of products, customers, industry segments, and geographic markets to emphasize more and, conversely, those to emphasize less? The answer is simple: to create a filter that will help employees make *consistent* and *logical* decisions on behalf of the company. And there are two types of decisions that will shape the "look" of the company over time.

The first is how resources are allocated. Most companies allocate resources through a budget mechanism. The difficulty with most budget systems is that they start at the lowest levels in the organization and creep their way up different silos. How the people at the lowest levels go about determining what they will accomplish in the next two or three years is by looking back at what *they have achieved in the last two to three years*–the numbers–and then projecting the numbers into the future while making minor adjustments for costs, inflation, and currency swings. This type of planning seeks to go forward by looking in the rear-view mirror. It does nothing to change the "look" of the company. Basically, it takes the company in its current state and extrapolates that state into the future yet does not advance the company's future ability to enhance its supremacy over its competitors.

The primary use of the strategic profile, then, is as a tool to ensure that people in the company allocate resources *strategically* around the organization. With the strategic profile in place, resources are allocated to items that look like those on the *more emphasis* side of the ledger rather than items that look like those on the *less emphasis* side. In other words, putting the organization's resources and energy in the areas where it can attain supremacy, as opposed to areas where it cannot.

The second type of decision that will shape the "look" of an organization over time is how opportunities are chosen. Once the profile is in place, the CEO can send a message advising the troops to pursue opportunities that look like items on the *more emphasis* side rather than opportunities that look like items on the *less emphasis* side.

How a company allocates resources or chooses opportunities are the two types of decisions that will determine the "look" of the business over time and the degree to which it can achieve supremacy. Which brings us to the next question: "How does management go about deciding on the line of demarcation between the items that should receive more emphasis and those that should receive less?" The answer to this important question lies in the fundamental concept of strategic supremacy: the *Driving Force.*

Chapter 7

Driving Force:
The Engine Of
Strategic Supremacy

The best way to determine if a CEO and the management team have a strategy is to observe them in meetings as they try to decide whether or not to pursue an opportunity. When we sat in on such meetings, what we observed was that management would put each opportunity through a hierarchy of different filters. The ultimate filter, however, was always whether there was a fit between the products, customers, and markets that the opportunity brought and *one* key component of the organization. If they found a fit there, they would feel comfortable with that opportunity, and would proceed with it. If they did not find a fit there, they would pass.

Different companies, however, looked for a *different* kind of fit. Some companies looked for a fit between similar products. Others were less concerned about the similarity of products than about a fit with the customer base. Still others were not interested in the similarity of products or of the customer base, but rather a fit with the technology involved, or a fit with its sales and marketing method, or its distribution system. Some quick examples.

What fit was Daimler looking for when it bought Chrysler? Obviously, the fit was one between similar products. Johnson & Johnson, on the other hand, looked for an entirely different kind of fit when it acquired Neutrogena creams and the clinical laboratories of Kodak, each bringing dramatically different products. The company was looking for a fit between the class of customers served–doctors, nurses, patients, and mothers–the heartbeat of J&J's strategy. 3M looked for still another fit when choosing opportunities. 3M did not care what the products were or who the customers were. What 3M did care about was whether there was a fit between the technology that the opportunity required and the technology–polymer chemistry–that lay at the root of 3M's strategy. If the technology fit, then 3M management felt comfortable in pursuing that opportunity.

Ten Strategic Areas

The next question that came to our minds was: "What are the areas of an organization that cause management to decide how to allocate resources or choose opportunities?" We discovered that each of the 400-plus companies we had worked with consisted of ten basic components.

- Every company offered a **product** or **service** for sale.
- Every company sold its product(s) or service(s) to a certain **class of customer** or **end user**.
- These customers or end users always resided in certain **categories of markets**.
- Every company employed **technology** in its product or service.
- Every company had a **production facility** located somewhere that had a certain amount of **capacity** or certain in-built **capabilities** in the making of a product or service.
- Every company used certain **sales** or **marketing methods** to acquire customers for its product or service.
- Every company employed certain **distribution methods** to get a product from its location to a customer's location.
- Every company made use of **natural resources** to one degree or another.
- Every company monitored its **size** and **growth** performance.
- Every company monitored its **return** or **profit** performance.

Two Key Messages

As a result of these observations, two key messages emerged. First, all ten areas exist in every company. Second, and more importantly, *one* of the ten areas tends to *dominate* the strategy of a company consistently over time. It is to favor or leverage this one area of the business time and again that determines how management allocates resources or chooses opportunities. In other words, one component of the business is the *engine* of the strategy–that company's so called DNA, or Driving Force. This Driving Force determines the array of products, customers, industries and geographic markets that management chooses to emphasize more and emphasize less.

Driving Force: Supremacy's Propeller

In order to explain this concept more clearly, one needs to look at an organization as a *body in motion.* Every organization, on any one day, is an organism that has movement and momentum and is going forward in some direction. Our thesis is that one of the ten components of a company's operation is the strategic engine behind the decisions that management makes. Some typical examples follow.

Defining the driving force.

Strategy Driven By Product

A company that is pursuing a product-driven strategy has deliberately decided to limit its strategy to a singular product and its derivatives. Therefore, all future products and the "current" product are linear, genetic extrapolations of the very first product that company ever made. In other words, the look, form, or function of the product stays constant over time. Examples are Coca-Cola (soda), Boeing (airplanes), Michelin (tires), Harley-Davidson (motorcycles), and many of the automobile manufacturers (GM; Toyota; Volkswagen).

Strategy Driven By User Or Customer Class

A company that is driven by a user or customer class has deliberately decided to restrict its strategy to a describable and circumscribable class of end users or customers (people). These end users or customers are the only ones the company serves. The company then identifies a common need of the user or customer class and responds with a wide array of genetically unrelated products. Examples are Johnson & Johnson (doctors, nurses, patients, and mothers), AARP (adults over 50), Playboy ("entertainment for *men*") and USAA (military officers).

Strategy Driven By Market Type Or Category

A company that is driven by market category has deliberately decided to limit its strategy to a describable marketplace or market type. The company identifies a common need among buyers in that market and then responds with a wide variety of genetically unrelated products. Examples are American *Hospital* Supply (now Allegiance) and Disney's concept of "wholesome entertainment for the *family.*"

Strategy Driven By Technology

A technology-driven company is rooted in some basic, hard technology such as chemistry or physics or some soft technology such as know-how or expertise. The company then goes looking for applications for its technology or expertise. Once it finds an application, the company develops a product that is infused with its technology for that application, and offers the new product to all the customers in that market with a similar application. While growing that business, the company goes around looking for another application to repeat the same process. Examples are Dupont (chemistry), 3M (polymers), and Intel (microprocessor architecture).

Strategy Driven By Production Capability Or Capacity

A company driven by production *capacity* is one which has a substantial investment in its production facility. The key phrase heard around the company is "keep it humming"–three shifts per day, seven days per week, 365 days per year. The strategy is to keep the production facility operating at a maximum level of capacity. Examples are steel companies, refineries, and pulp-and-paper companies.

A company driven by production *capability* has incorporated some distinctive capabilities into its production process that allows it to do things to its products that its competitors have difficulty duplicating. As a result, when the company goes looking for opportunities, it restricts its search to opportunities where these capabilities can be exploited. Specialty converters in a variety of industries are good examples.

Strategy Driven By Sales Or Marketing Method

When a strategy is driven by a sales or marketing method, the company has a unique or distinctive method of selling to its customers. All the opportunities it pursues must utilize that selling method. Examples are companies that sell door-to-door (Avon, Mary Kay, and Amway), direct-response companies (Dell and K-tel), and catalog companies (L.L. Bean and Land's End). A recent addition is amazon.com, whose strategy is to use the Internet to sell a wide array of consumer products.

Strategy Driven By Distribution Method

A company driven by a distribution method has a unique or distinctive approach of moving tangible or intangible things from one place to another. All the opportunities such a company pursues must optimize that distribution method. Examples are Wal-Mart, FedEx, Home Depot, Staples, and Nextel.

Strategy Driven By Natural Resources

A company whose entire purpose is the pursuit and exploitation of oil, gas, ore, gold, timber or other resources can be said to be pursuing a natural resource-driven strategy. Examples are Exxon, Shell, Newmont Gold, and Anglo-American Mining.

Strategy Driven By Size Or Growth

A company driven by size or growth is usually a conglomerate of unrelated businesses. Its sole strategic interest is growth and size for their own sake.

Strategy Driven By Return Or Profit

A company whose sole strategic focus is a minimum level of return or profit is also a conglomerate of unrelated businesses. The best example during the 1970's was ITT under Harold Geneen. His dictum of "an increase in quarterly earnings, every quarter, from every unit, regardless what" led ITT into 276 different businesses. These businesses were deliberately kept separate so that when any one unit missed its profit target for three consecutive quarters, it was gone in the fourth! Other examples today are AlliedSignal and General Electric, where Jack Welch's dictum of an 18 percent ROA has landed GE into everything from light bulbs to television networks to financial services to turbines and aircraft engines.

Key Strategic Questions

When we take a client through our Strategic Thinking Process, we have the CEO and the management team debate three key questions.

QUESTION 1: Which component of your business is currently *driving* your strategy and has made you look as you look today in terms of current products, customers, and markets?

If there are ten people in the room, how many answers do you think we get? Ten and sometimes more. The reason is simple. Each person has a different perception as to which component of the business is the Driving Force behind the company's strategy. These different interpretations lead to different visions of where the organization is headed. The difficulty, while this is going on, is that each member of the team makes decisions that pull the company left and right, so the company zigzags its way forward without establishing supremacy in any one sandbox.

The methodology we bring to bear at DPI encourages management to look back at the history of decisions they have made and, by doing so, recognize a pattern. Typically, most of their decisions were made to favor *one* component of the business. Thus, the management team recognizes the *current* Driving Force behind their *current* strategy.

QUESTION 2: Which component of the company *should* be the Driving Force behind the company's strategy in the *future?*

This question is more important, because it indicates that the company's future strategy should not be an extrapolation of the current strategy. Any strategy needs to accommodate the environment the company will encounter in the future, and that environment could be very different from the one encountered in the past.

QUESTION 3: What impact will this Driving Force have on the choices the company must make regarding future products, future customers, and future markets?

The Driving Force the company chooses as the engine of its strategy will determine the choices its management makes as to the products, customers, and markets that they *will* and *will not emphasize* in the future. These choices will shape the profile of the company over time. Each

Driving Force will cause management to make very different choices that will make the company look very differently than the way it looks today. In other words, just as your personal DNA determines what you look like and why you look differently from other people, the same is true for your corporate DNA. Which component of the company you decide to make the DNA of its strategy will determine what that company will eventually look like and why it looks differently from its competitors.

Fundamental Concept Of Strategic Supremacy

The concept of Driving Force–to us at DPI–is one that is *fundamental* for any successful CEO to understand. It is the recognition and understanding, by all members of the management team, of that *one* predominant component of the business–its Driving Force–that will allow the organization to formulate a strategy based on a *distinctive* and *sustainable advantage* that can give it supremacy over its competition.

Getting agreement on a single Driving Force is not an easy task. The following questions raised by CEOs and their management teams reveal the reasons why.

Does Your Strategy Suffer From The "Sybil Syndrome"?

"I can think of four or five strategic areas present in our business and they are of equal importance." In other words, there are *multiple* Driving Forces at work in the company. When we present the concept of Driving Force to CEOs for the first time, this is usually the first reaction that we get. We call it the "Sybil Syndrome." Do you remember the movie *Sybil*, about a woman with multiple personalities? Do you think that she had an easy time living with herself? Of course not! Every morning when she awoke, she did not know who she was. The same can be true of a company.

If multiple strategic areas are at the root of a company's strategy, and these strategies are regarded as equally important, the organization will develop multiple personalities and won't be able to tolerate itself. The following strategy statement, from a real company, is a good example.

"The Corporation strives to be a profitable and growing global manufacturer and marketer of value-added chemicals, an innovative supplier of niche life insurance and annuity products, and an increasingly significant force in the pharmaceutical industry."

The company? The Ethyl Corporation. When was the last time you saw this company mentioned as having supremacy in any of these sandboxes? In fact, the company had such difficulty living with itself that it eventually divided into *four* separate public companies.

Does Your Strategy Suffer From Schizophrenia?

"If there cannot be multiple business areas driving our strategy, then I can identify two components in our company, equally important, that work in tandem." We call this the "schizophrenic strategy." One day you are in *this* mode, the next day you are in *that* mode. And the company zigzags its way forward, bouncing from one questionable opportunity to another.

Our contention is that, at any one moment in time, every organization has a *single* business component that is the Driving Force behind its strategy. Until members of the management team determine which component that is, they will have frequent disagreements over the allocation of resources and the choice of sound opportunities to pursue.

Is Profit Not The Single Purpose Of A Company?

It is a well-known fact that people must eat in order to survive. If they don't eat, they will die, guaranteed! But surely the purpose of life is not eating. Surely, there must be another purpose to life other than eating, although people must eat every day.

The same line of thinking applies to a company. Most businesses have another purpose in life, a Driving Force other than profit, although whatever that Driving Force is, every strategy must produce a profit. If a company is not profitable, it will die, guaranteed! However, profit is the *result* of the strategy, not its *objective*. Profit tells you whether your strategy is working or not, but profit is not usually *the* strategy.

Isn't Any Strategy Subject To Darwinism?

Doesn't every strategy evolve over time? In other words, doesn't a company start with a certain Driving Force and evolve naturally to a second Driving Force and then eventually to a third, and so forth? Could you not start as product-driven, then go to technology and then to customer class? Isn't there a natural evolution over time?

The answer, generally, is no. A good strategy stays in place and works for an organization over a long period of time. Take, for example, Mercedes' concept of the "best-engineered car." This strategy was first articulated in 1888 and, from then until today, that concept has produced a profit every single year. The same is true of Wal-Mart, Johnson & Johnson, Disney, and several others. In fact, we would propose that the opposite is also true. If you feel that your strategy needs to change frequently, that is a clear signal you don't have one!

Are There Any Legitimate Reasons For Changing The Driving Force?

There are two instances when you might want to shift the strategy and direction of your organization by deliberately changing the underlying Driving Force of your current strategy.

The first occurs when your current strategy runs out of growth. Growth, like profit, is a "given" in business. Any company must grow to perpetuate itself. Therefore, when your strategy starts sputtering and runs out of growth, you have a *legitimate* reason to sit down with your team and debate whether the time has come to change the historical Driving Force behind your current strategy. One company that has been in this mode for the last ten years is Playboy. Its long-time strategy of providing "entertainment for men" with a very specific profile (young adult male, single, middle to upper income) led the company to everything from magazines to casinos. The strategy worked for 30 years. However, in the 1980s, the absolute number of young adult single males began to diminish as a result of evolving demographics, and Playboy's strategy started running out of growth and came to a quick halt. Since then, Playboy has been looking for a strategy that will prove as good as the one that worked for over 30 years.

The second situation arises when you look down the horizon and see a death threat. In other words, there is something at the root of the company's strategy that could make the current Driving Force obsolete. This is another, extremely *legitimate* reason for calling a meeting to explore changing the strategy and direction of the company. Such might be the case for a company like Johnson & Johnson. If anyone–that is, anyone other than J&J–ever invented a *wellness* pill, that would be the end of J&J's strategy of satisfying the "health needs of doctors, nurses, patients, and mothers." Then you would see J&J look for other customer groups to satisfy with radically different products than today's. J&J executives, on the other hand, have looked down that horizon and don't see obsolescence as a very high probability, so they will stay with their current Driving Force and strategy.

Does Your Strategy Succumb To Seduction?

Alongside these two legitimate reasons for changing the Driving Force and strategy of a company are factors that cause the strategy to change by *accident and not by design.* Management gets seduced by opportunities! An opportunity comes along and management, looking only at the numbers, concludes that it cannot afford not to be in that business. The company then pursues the opportunity, because of the numbers, only to discover later that the opportunity has another Driving Force at its root. Before long, opportunity starts pulling the whole company off course.

When Is Seduction At Its Peak?

A company's management succumbs to seduction when its current strategy is so successful that it is generating more cash than the business needs. And the company starts accumulating excess cash. This is a situation that happened to Daimler Benz, as it was known in the mid-1980s. From 1980 to 1985, the company accumulated a cash hoard of over $8 billion that had nothing to do with the sale of cars but rather to swings in the currency markets. Rather than keep the money for a rainy day, the then-CEO decided to go on an acquisition binge; the company soon found itself the proud owner of AEG, Dornier, and MBB–all basket cases. Trying to fix these businesses caused management to take its eye off the ball–the car business. The shift in focus gave BMW the opening to concentrate on taking market share away from its major competitor which is exactly what it did. It took Daimler Benz over ten years to rid itself of these albatrosses and refocus itself on the car business. The company finally acquired Chrysler in 1998, an acquisition it should have made years earlier, when Chrysler could have been bought for a song.

Are Some Driving Forces Inherently Incompatible?

The answer is yes. A good example is Compaq. During the 1990's under the direction of CEO Eckhard Pfeiffer, the company soared on its product-driven strategy–"business PCs". The strategy was so successful that management convinced itself that it could run any computer company. So when Digital Equipment Corporation (DEC) ran into difficulties, Compaq jumped in and bought DEC outright. Compaq quickly discovered that it had become owner of a company with a very different strategy–"complex information systems for corporations"–a concept driven by a market category. Instead of the relatively simple business of selling and distributing personal computers in different-colored boxes, Compaq now found itself in the business of providing large, multitask computers that required proprietary software and on-going service, elements that PCs don't need. Here were two very different *businesses*–and, unfortunately, with two conflicting Driving Forces and strategies. It doesn't matter how smart management thinks it is. If two Driving Forces are *inherently incompatible,* they will never be made to work.

This conflict turned out to be fatal for Pfeiffer. Six months after the merger became official, the company announced earnings that were substantially below Wall Street's expectations. Pfeiffer was quickly ousted by the board's Chairman, Benjamin Rosen. At the press conference announcing the dismissal, Rosen stated, "Compaq's strategy is sound. Execution is the hang-up. We need to execute better." Compaq's customers thought otherwise. "I don't know what they stand for anymore," said one. In our view, Compaq had adopted an incoherent strategy. And just as its customers recognized Compaq's strategic incoherence, so did its employees. Thus, the reason for poor execution. People cannot be expected to execute well a strategy that is flawed from the word "go."

Strategy By Design, Not By Accident

The purpose of the Strategic Thinking Process is to help a company's CEO and management team make *conscious* decisions whose rationale and underlying logic are clearly understood. Understanding what the company does best–its *Driving Force* and making it the engine of its strategy –is *the* key skill of management. Once management agrees on the "engine", they are then able to formulate and deploy a distinctive strategy which can be leveraged to achieve supremacy over its competitors.

Which area should be the *Driving Force*?

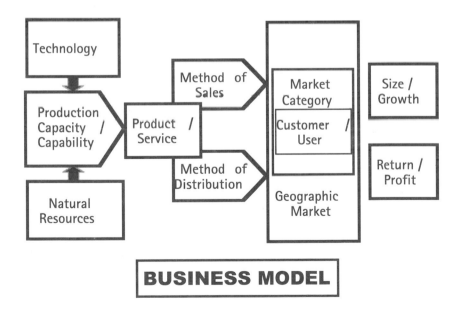

BUSINESS MODEL

Focus, Focus, Focus

The key to supremacy is simple: "Singularity of purpose, total dedication to it and no deviation from it." This mantra demands that the strategy be kept strong and healthy which, in turn, requires the nurturing of what we call "Areas of Excellence". Which Driving Force is chosen as the "strategic engine" will greatly alter the "Areas of Excellence" that a company must continually enhance if it wants to amplify the supremacy gap over its competitors. Understanding the relationship between the Driving Force and the corresponding Areas of Excellence allows management to deploy the company's energy and resources and enable it to *focus, focus, focus*. The interview that follows is a good illustration of this concept.

Charles Foster
Chairman & Chief Executive Officer

Ted Chandler
Senior Executive Vice President

Taking Title To A Brand New Game

Title insurance. To most of us it's just one of those details that come up in the blur of closing a real estate transaction. But, to LandAmerica, it's their bread and butter. Or was–until a startling revelation occurred as the \vcompany's managers went through DPI's Strategic Thinking and e-Strategy Processes.

Currently, LandAmerica is the second largest U.S. supplier of title insurance policies at about $2 billion in revenues. The company is the product of the merging of two large competitors, Lawyer's Title and the Commonwealth family of companies in February of 1998.

As mergers go, this one went quite well, as CEO Charlie Foster describes: "There were some good cultural fits, and we brought them together. We went through a year of a robust economy, which helped, but then the world had been changing and continued to change. I believe our entire management team was looking for more cohesion than we had been able to articulate. We had completed a lot of projects with regard to the merger and systems and organizational structures needed to be changed, but we weren't sending a consistent internal message regarding growth strategies in the face of emerging technologies. We were just saying, here we're two companies that used to do something, how do we do it together? We got by that and there was this companywide hunger, this need, this management imperative, to be clearer about the future." In addition, there was a pressing need to deal with some fundamental shifts in the industry. Other mergers. The effects of the Internet. The very nature of how real estate transactions were being done. How would they react? Could they find a way *not* to be reactive, but to be more in charge of their own destiny?

As Foster explains, "It really boiled down to the competitive environment of what was going on in the industry, with how real estate transactions come down. The mortgage originators began to behave differently because of consolidations and capabilities afforded them through what I'll call e-commerce or the Internet. There were consolidations going on in our industry and talk of further consolidation. But the state of our business really had to be characterized as one that was more *reactive* than proactive. We were dealing with the world as it was shifting, and *responding* to it. Before starting the Strategic Thinking Process, I think that's a fair characterization."

Adds Senior Executive Vice President Ted Chandler, "We began to see the limitations of our historical focus on being a single-product vendor of title insurance. We were concerned that this singular focus in a rapidly shifting market positioned us more on the *periphery* of the action than we used to be, and than we wanted to be. We saw the opportunities, but we were not clear on how we should alter our positioning to take advantage of them."

The management team decided to look for objective outside assistance to work out a strategy. But unsatisfactory results from previous encounters with "traditional" content-based consultants led them to look for another solution. DPI's Strategic Thinking Process seemed to fit their needs.

"We first concluded that we would like to have a facilitator-enhanced process," Chandler says. "We had experience with consultants that came in and attempted to provide domain expertise, but we knew that the real answers were locked up within us. We were looking for a set of professionals who could help us pull those ideas out. Really, the DPI Process, led by a facilitator who transfers the process skills that you need to continue and give momentum to the process, was exactly what we were looking for."

Adds Charlie Foster, "If I could characterize it another way, we were responding to the outside world, including shareholders and the investment community. And we were, I guess fairly, self-assessing ourselves as having a lack of clarity. And we needed a clarity of purpose first of all–what it is we want to do, what our mission really *should* be–and then clarity of thought as to how to approach that goal, that objective of getting *the purpose.* So we were looking for more of a discipline, something that would be continuous, not *the answer* by the *guru du jour.*"

They gathered a LandAmerica management team from a cross-section of locations and disciplines, twenty-five in all, to participate. Right from the start the Strategic Thinking concept clicked.

"The reaction from our people was very positive," Chandler says. "I think there was a desire for this. We, like most companies, had a strategy. We were executing on a strategy but it tended to be more of an implicit strategy that was not being aggressively communicated beyond the executive suite. And the reason is, as Charlie said, there was a bit of a lack of clarity as to how boldly we should be taking advantage of these opportunities. When we brought the people together for the work session, I think there was a real buy-in that it was appropriate, and needed."

Despite the fact that the participants had come from many parts of the company and country, the process quickly got them on the same page and moving toward a surprising conclusion. It became immediately apparent that the company might make a major change of direction, and Driving Force–creating an opportunity to drastically change the game in their sandbox.

As Chandler explains, "Because this business is largely locally driven and because real estate laws are different, and customs and practices are different, when you pull these people together you find that it takes a while to talk the same language. This is because the business, even though it's under the rubric of title insurance, is actually executed differently depending on your geographic market. So the effort to identify the Driving Force brought on a lot of discussion. And we actually, I think, are unusual among companies that have gone through the DPI process because we have *changed* our Driving Force. After we identified our current Driving Force as Product–title insurance policies–we realized we could really *change the game* if we moved to a *new* Driving Force–User Class."

To put a finer point on it, they would be moving away from being simply a title insurance company, and moving toward providing a wide range of services, all related to the real estate transaction. Instead of selling a single piece of the puzzle, they would eventually manage the entire transaction–a radically different business model.

"The simple truth of the matter," says Charlie Foster, "is that we had been very oriented towards something called a title insurance policy, which, if you peeled it back, had 95% *information* value versus 5% *insurance* value. But our current thesis is to try to respond to what the customer *really* wants. And the customer, no matter if it's a lender or a realtor, a builder-developer or an attorney–our basic customer sets–what we think they want is a facilitated transaction, not just the title insurance. And so we're putting ourselves in a position to be that concierge, to be the facilitator, to provide that *seamless transaction.* And we're starting to call ourselves a *transaction manager,* as a simple phrase, as opposed to a title insurance fulfiller."

"The primary piece of it is that we had to get away from thinking of ourselves as just a title insurance company," Chandler says. "So our sandbox is that *we proactively provide services in the information, assurance, fiduciary, and settlement segments of the real estate business. And we intend to be the preeminent provider of seamless transactions and value-added knowledge through economical, time sensitive and customized solutions.* That combined statement of our future strategic profile does a number of things. It focuses people on the fact that when we talk about *information, assurance, fiduciary, and settlement,* then *title insurance* tucks into *assurance.* It's just one of a series of guarantee products that we can provide. And when we speak to a sandbox that encompasses providing the information needs of the real estate industry, we're talking about, in fact, a *very* large market opportunity. That articulation of the sandbox and aggressive development of multiple products in that area coupled with our intent *to be the preeminent provider of seamless transactions,* leads us into an e-strategy emphasis and the need to build a different profile than we had been pursuing."

A change of Driving Force mandates a corresponding change in the Areas of Excellence to be developed and nurtured. LandAmerica's people do not perceive this to be a major problem, as these areas are not entirely new to the company's culture. It simply means a change of emphasis.

As Chandler sees it, "Our main Area of Excellence is Market Knowledge, which is really an aggregation of local market knowledge. To support that we will also need to concentrate more on Information Management and Technology. Even though we're in the 'insurance business,' that is very much misleading. We're an information management company and that is really our business. And then thirdly, is Internet Technology, and that is a skill set, not just purchased goods. It is an area of focus, and it is highlighted under our future strategic profile management because we need to leverage it to a significantly greater degree."

To get their arms around the role that the Internet might play in the future, they decided to use DPI's e-Strategy Process, again with very surprising results.

Says Foster, "We didn't realize, going in, the kinds of things we'd come up with and how central they would be to our new strategy. I looked at it as a scenario of 'Gee, I don't know enough; this is education. Let's do it!' You know, you have these natural anxieties and fears that somebody knows something you don't know. So that's why we went into that process. The almost immediate outcome of that is, now we don't even call this e-strategy. *This is just strategy.* It was its own separate project at the outset. In fact now it's one of our major Critical Issues to the overall development of strategy. So we're attempting to learn and to build and develop strategy based upon what I call the evolution of Internet based commerce."

"We had, in our previous, fragmented approach to the Internet, responded to one of our customer sets by building a part of our company, which we called LandAmerica One-Stop, to try to respond to what the customer was saying. But we were doing it looking through the eyeglasses of a title insurer. So we hadn't thought of everything. In fact, we weren't, from a technology standpoint, very far along in terms of connectivity. We had struggled with that. Because of the DPI Process, we immediately recognized the need to look at it in the broader context."

That broader context, of course, was the new, more expansive strategy the company had embarked on. Given that their products are essentially information products and that the thousands of potential customers are located literally everywhere, e-commerce would play a central role as the concept developed.

The e-Strategy Process allowed them to create a realistic and comprehensive design for an e-commerce solution that would precisely fit their new business model–complete with definitions of specific applications and their requirements. What really made the whole e-commerce concept gel, though, was the transformation they saw take place through the "Killer.com" segment of the process.

"Part of what we had done during the Process was to engage ourselves in two or three exercises. But one of them was much more than an exercise, it was something about building a whole new model. And through the Killer.Com we came up with an approach that turned the light on and said, you know, this sounds exotic but it really is what we're trying to do. It's just a way of explaining it, of giving it a complete definition," Foster states.

The result is the game-changing "Transaction Manager" concept, brought to market, in part, by the Internet portal described in more detail in Chapter 5. This breakthrough model will take years to bring to fruition, but LandAmerica wasted no time getting started. Within weeks, they made a strategic acquisition that would supply a critical piece of the new business.

Chandler explains: "We, almost immediately out of the box, after having our phase-two session, once our future strategic profile was set, once the strategic filter was delivered, applied that filter to several pressing opportunities. We zeroed in on this one particular target company, called Primis. We very boldly acquired the company, and we have incorporated that business into one of our most important market segments. So there was this absolute direct, not indirect, linkage between the development of that Strategic Filter and us pulling the trigger on a major initiative.

"Primis embodies our movement into this transaction management space in a key market segment. What we got with that company was a whole array of valuation products we were not offering and market knowledge of where innovation was needed. We also were able to get technology that was specific to those products. But what we had, and what we saw, and what has proved out is that that acquired technology was readily adaptable to be our primary e-commerce front-end with respect to this one very large market segment. So, when we bought Primis we merged it into one of our companies that was operating in the same market but didn't have the same set of tools. And combined we are very, very well positioned to be the transaction manager for our largest, most demanding customers.

"I can actually say, unequivocally, that we would not have bought Primis but for the DPI Process. I mean that just flat out, because prior to DPI, we were not looking to expand into, essentially, another line of business–the valuation products line of business. And even if we had been, we would not have done it at this level of financial commitment."

Because of the complexity of the new LandAmerica business model, it will take some time to develop it and mold it into a complete, integrated operation. Primis is an important piece of the puzzle. Yet despite the challenges inherent in creating a new game, Foster and his team are confident that the concept is sound and that the market is moving toward using this type of service. The journey has also completely changed their perception of the game, the rules and the nature of competition in their space.

"We haven't completed them yet," says Chandler, "but the transaction management tactics that we're bringing to the table will have the effect of changing the rules. We're doing business in a way that's different than any of our natural competitors. We are actually, counter-intuitively positioning ourselves so that we will even sell our competitors' products. We are moving into the transaction intersection to manage the transaction, and, if our customer wants to use our competitor for the title order, then we're going to do that. So what changes the rules of play is that all of a sudden when a customer chooses us, they're not making a choice on one major title company versus another major title company where the differences across the country may not always be apparent or real. They're making a choice that they want a manager of that transaction who will then use the fulfillment entities that are best in class–best in class being defined by the customer or in the absence of being defined by the customer, defined as quicker, better, cheaper. This will fundamentally change the game and the rules of play because we do not see our other traditional competitors positioning themselves in a way that they would forego the title insurance order.

"As a result, we are less obsessed with our traditional competitors than we were before. I think one of the benefits of going through the DPI Process is that you become more confident in the direction of the company and therefore you're less reactive to their 'me-too' type strategies. And the other piece of this is that we recognize that our traditional competitors, in this brave new world, are perhaps not our *real* competitors. That comes out of the Killer.Com evaluation. So we are much more going to go in *our own direction*, full of 'competitors be damned,' than we were prior to the DPI Process."

Throughout the next couple of years, a new type of company will emerge, although pieces of the model may change as ideas are tested and adjusted to fit the evolving marketplace. Says CEO Foster, "We have come up with what we think is a pretty good game plan. Now it isn't proven out and it changes from time to time. In fact one of the beauties of this whole DPI effort is the fact that it is a continuum. Strategic thinking is just that, a continuum of thinking."

Where would they be had they continued on their former course? Foster puts it succinctly: "We probably would have been much more on the target end of the range than the shooting end."

Chapter 8

Areas Of Excellence: Amplifying The Supremacy Gap

Jeff Bezos, the CEO of amazon.com, eloquently articulated our concept of Strategic Supremacy with this statement:

> "Barnes & Noble and Borders are having trouble because it is hard to pursue me-too strategies online. In book retailing, amazon.com still does the best job, and not by a little. The gap between us and our competitors is significant and grows every quarter."

There are two interesting parts to this statement. First, the recognition that me-too strategies are not worth the paper they are written on and that only a strategy that is distinctive and sets you apart from your competitors will enable you to attain supremacy over them. The second interesting part of this statement is the notion that the "gap" between a company and its competitors can amplify over time. This "supremacy gap" is created and can amplify over time by the cultivation of what we call *areas of excellence.*

An *area of excellence* is a specific *skill or capability* which a company *deliberately* nurtures to a higher level of proficiency than any other competitor because it is their superiority in these two or three capabilities that keeps their strategy strong and healthy and widens the supremacy gap over their competitors.

Some CEOs understand this concept and know exactly what these areas of excellence are that give the company its strategic advantage over its competitors.

David Glass, the recently retired CEO of Wal-Mart, said:

> "Our distribution facilities are the key to our success.
> If we do anything better than other folks, that's it."

Knowing that, Glass invested over a billion dollars during his reign on sophisticated computer systems to maintain and increase that supremacy gap.

Fred Smith, CEO of FedEx, also knows what contributes to its supremacy over its competitors:

> "The main difference between us and our
> competitors is that we have more capacity to
> track, trace and control items in the system."

What we discovered, however, is that the Areas of Excellence needed vary greatly from one Driving Force to another.

In other words, each different component of the business you select as the engine of your strategy will demand *excellence* in a very different set of capabilities. Let's explore some examples.

Determining The Strategic Capabilities
That Amplify Supremacy

Product-Driven Strategy

A product/service-driven company survives on the quality of its product or service. Witness the automobile wars. Who's winning? The Japanese. Why have Americans been buying Japanese cars and even been willing to pay premium prices for the last 40 years? The answer is simple: The

Japanese make better cars. The bottom line for a product-driven strategy is: best product wins!

One area of excellence, therefore, is *product development.* Compared to U.S. cars, Japanese cars of the late 1950s (when cars from Japan came onto the market) were far inferior. But Japanese car manufacturers understood well that "best car wins" and they strove to improve the product–to make it better and better–to the extent that Japanese cars eventually surpassed the quality of U.S. cars.

A second area of excellence is *service.* IBM, which also pursues a product-driven strategy, is well aware of this requirement. Ask IBM clients what they admire most about IBM, and 99 out of 100 will say they admire its service capability. IBM deliberately invests more resources in its service function than any of its competitors, and thus has a considerable edge in response time and infrequency of product failures.

In a product-driven mode, you amplify your supremacy by cultivating excellence in *product development* and *product service.*

Market Category/User Class-Driven Strategy

An organization that is market category or user class-driven must also cultivate excellence to optimize its strategic supremacy, but in dramatically different areas.

A market /user class-driven company has placed its destiny in the hands of a *market category or a class of users.* Therefore, to survive and prosper, it must know its user class or market category better than any competitor. *Market* or *user research*, then, is one area of excellence. The company must know everything there is to know about its market or user in order to quickly detect any changes in habits, demographics, likes and dislikes. Proctor & Gamble interviews consumers (particularly homemakers) over two million times per year in an attempt to anticipate trends that can be converted into product opportunities.

A second area of excellence for a market / user class-driven company is *user loyalty.* Through a variety of means, these companies, over time, build customer loyalty to the company's products or brands. Then they trade on this loyalty. Over time, Johnson & Johnson has convinced its customers that its products are "safe." And it will not let anything infringe on the loyalty it has developed because of this guarantee. Whenever a Johnson & Johnson product might prove to be a hazard to a person's health, it is immediately removed from the market.

Production Capacity/Capability-Driven Strategy

When there is a glut of paper on the market, the first thing a paper company does is lower the price. Therefore, to survive during the period of low prices, one has to have the lowest costs of any competitor. To achieve this, *manufacturing or plant efficiency* is a required area of excellence. This is why paper companies are forever investing their profits in their mills—to make them more and more efficient. An industry that has lost sight of this notion is the U.S. steel industry. By not improving their plants, they have lost business to the Italians and Japanese, who have done so. One notable exception in the United States is Nucor, which has done very well because it has the lowest costs of any steel mill, including the Japanese and Italian mills. As a result, Nucor's revenues and profits have consistently improved.

A second area of excellence for the production capacity-driven strategy is *substitute marketing*. Capacity-driven companies excel at substituting what comes off their machines for other things. The paper people are trying to substitute paper for plastic; the plastic people are trying to substitute plastic for aluminum; concrete for steel. The same is true in the transportation industry where bus companies are trying to replace trains, and trains—the airlines, and so forth.

A production capability-driven company is one that has built special capabilities into its production process which allow it to make products with features that are difficult for its competitors to duplicate. It then looks for opportunities where these capabilities can be exploited.

Job shops and specialty printers are examples. As a result, these companies are always looking to add to or enhance these distinctive production capabilities, because herein resides their competitive advantage.

Technology/Know-How-Driven Strategy

A company that is technology-driven uses technology as its edge. Thus, an area of excellence required to win under this strategy is *research,* either basic or applied. Sony, for example, spends 10 percent of its sales on research, which is 2 or 3 percent more than any competitor. Its motto, "research is the difference," is proof that the company's management recognizes the need to excel in this area.

By pushing the technology further than any competitor, new products and new markets will emerge. Technology-driven companies usually *create* markets rather than respond to needs, and they usually follow their technology wherever it leads them.

A second area of excellence for technology-driven companies is *applications marketing.* Technology-driven companies seem to have a knack for finding applications for their technology that call for highly differentiated products. For example, 3M has used its coating technology to develop Post-it® note pads and some 60,000 other products.

Sales/Marketing Method-Driven Strategy

The prosperity of a sales method-driven company depends on the reach and effectiveness of its selling method. Dell, whose Driving Force is its direct response selling method, has the best web site of all companies which use the Internet as their selling method.

The second area of excellence needed to succeed with this strategy is improving the *effectiveness* of the selling method. Door-to-door companies are constantly training their salespeople in product knowledge, product demonstration, and selling skills. Growth and profits come from improving volume through the diversity and effectiveness of its sales method.

Distribution Method-Driven Strategy

To win the war while pursuing a distribution method-driven strategy, you must first have the *most effective* distribution method. As a result, you offer only products and services that use or enhance your distribution system. Second, you must always look to ways to optimize the *effectiveness,* either in cost or value, of that system. That is your edge. You should also be on the lookout for any form of distribution that could bypass or make your distribution method obsolete.

Both Federal Express and Wal-Mart are good examples of distribution method-driven companies. They are constantly striving to improve the efficiency of their respective distribution systems.

Natural Resource-Driven Strategy

Successful resource-driven companies excel at doing just that–*exploring* and finding the type of resources they are engaged in. Exxon considers itself to be the best at "exploring for oil and gas," and it does this better than any competitor. It was the recognition of this fact that led Exxon to drop its office equipment division. There's not much oil and gas to be found there, plus that kind of venture requires excellence in areas Exxon does not possess.

John Bookout, ex-CEO of Shell USA, is a good example of a strategist who understood his company's areas of excellence. Shell's particular expertise is "enhanced oil recovery in offshore waters deeper than 600 feet." In this area, Shell has few rivals, as Bookout explained. In 1983, Shell drilled a project called Bullwinkle in the Gulf of Mexico at a depth of 1350 feet. Outsiders thought the project was too risky, particularly since Shell did not spread the risk by taking other partners in on the deal. "You can't believe how easy that decision was," he says. "It took us 30 minutes in the boardroom." The reason? Bookout was banking on Shell's area of excellence in deep water recovery.

This area of excellence has enabled Shell to paralyze its competitors. Shell recently announced major discoveries in the Gulf of Mexico that are estimated to contain a minimum of four billion barrels of oil. Even its competitors recognize this superiority. As Amoco CEO, Laurance Fuller, admits: "When it comes to deep water drilling, Shell is out in front of the industry."

Size/Growth Or Return/Profit-Driven Strategy

Companies that choose either a size/growth-driven or a return/ profit-driven strategy require excellence in financial management. One such area is *portfolio management.* This means proficiency at moving assets around in order to maximize the size/growth or return/profit of the entire organization.

A second area of excellence is *information systems.* These companies usually have a corporate "Big Brother" group that constantly monitors the performance of its various divisions and as soon as a problem is detected, an attempt is made quickly to correct or expunge it so that the financial damage can be kept to a minimum.

Importance Of Areas Of Excellence

Why are areas of excellence an integral part of strategic thinking supremacy? No company has the resources to develop skills equally in all areas. Therefore, another strategic decision that management must wrestle with, once the Driving Force has been identified, is to clearly identify those two or three skills that are critical and to give those areas *preferential* treatment. In good times, these areas receive additional resources; in bad times, you cut everywhere else, but you do not trim your Areas of Excellence.

A company, therefore, has two key strategic decisions to make if it wishes to succeed. First, it must determine which strategic area will give it strategic supremacy and be the Driving Force of its strategy. Second, it must decide what areas of excellence it must cultivate to enhance its supremacy. These areas of excellence should receive preferential treatment—fueled with more resources in order to develop a level of proficiency greater than any competitor. Once resources are diverted elsewhere, proficiency diminishes and the company loses its supremacy over its competitors.

Too often, organizations are distracted from what has made them successful. The most successful organizations are the ones in which the leader and senior management clearly understand their *Driving Force* and fuel the key areas of excellence required for success with more resources each year than they give to other areas. They then pursue their strategy with total dedication and without allowing any competitor to attain the same level of excellence in those few key capabilities. As Benjamin Disraeli so clearly noted many decades ago, "The secret to success is constancy of purpose." And, as Lewis Preston the ex-CEO of J.P. Morgan, one of the world's most successful banks, said about the firm he headed: "We aren't likely to deviate radically from the clear strategic path we have been on since the days of the first Morgan partners."

Knowing what strategic area drives your organization and the areas of excellence required to support that strategy is essential to understanding which strategic weapon will give you a distinct and sustainable advantage in the marketplace. Our experience has clearly shown that any strategy can work, but that no company can pursue more than one strategy at any one moment in time.

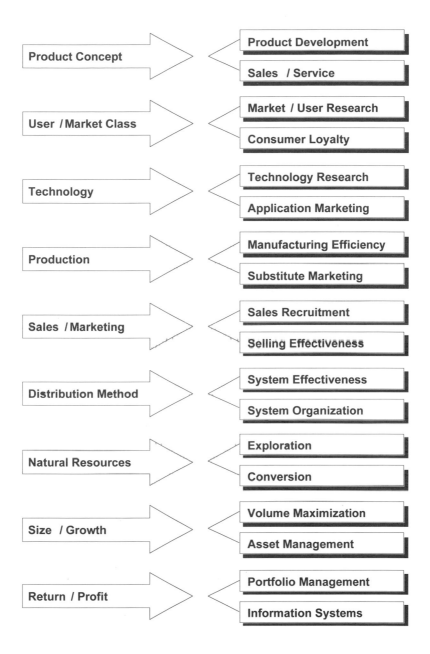

Determining the strategic capability of an organization is a key concept of Strategic Thinking.

Rak Kumar

Chief Executive Officer
Professional Division

Supremacy^2

Judo experts have always known that size doesn't matter. In fact with the right strategy, small size can be used as an *advantage* as business competitors vie for supremacy. As this story illustrates, a smaller combatant may be able to use its agility and strategic focus as weapons so powerful that it can topple and defeat larger competitors.

An undaunted commitment to this principle enabled a small, specialized printer manufacturer to leverage its Driving Force and Areas of Excellence so effectively that it not only defeated two much larger competitors, but also ran them *completely out of business*. Says Rak Kumar, CEO of Gretag Professional Imaging, "The only way you can beat the bigger players is by clearly understanding the sandbox you're playing in and changing the game in order to dominate that sandbox. You need to understand the whole concept of Driving Force and the one or two capabilities you must excel at–your Areas of Excellence–because you have limited resources and you need to know where to use those resources to strengthen these Areas of Excellence. That's the only way to win."

And win they have, as dedication to this simple credo has enabled Kumar's company to grow from $25 million in sales to $130 million in four years, with 30% annual growth predicted going forward. This, despite the fact that they were playing in a sandbox dominated by much larger companies–divisions of Xerox and Lockheed–that dwarfed them in size. Here's how it happened, as Kumar recounts this David and Goliath (actually David and Goliath and Goliath's bigger brother) tale.

"Back in 1996 we were a small company, called Raster Graphics, growing at about 25% a year. We make what we call printers for wide format imaging. That means we make printers for displays on the side of a bus or a Macy's window or a billboard," Kumar explains. "But when you have only about $25 million in revenue, you have limited resources, and we had very large companies as competitors. We were competing with Calcomp, a $400 million Lockheed division, and a division of Xerox that was at about $200 million at that time. Our big challenge was, as a small business with a good growth rate and good technology, what should we focus on? What should our strategy be over the next three to five years to continue to build the business at that rate and not get killed by giants such as the Xeroxes and the Lockheeds of the world?"

To assist the management team in making these crucial decisions, they enlisted the help of DPI and its Strategic Thinking Process. The DPI approach appealed to them because of its participatory nature.

"We looked at all the traditional BCG-type models, and we felt that there are two approaches to developing strategy. One approach is getting outside people to *tell* you what to do. At the root of the *other* approach, as Mike Robert always says, is the concept that the people who know your business best are the people *on your own team* and that they should create their own strategy. So, working with DPI was really an attempt on our part to get some help, and get the whole team to sit down together and come up with a game plan that made sense for our size of company and the environment we're living in," says Kumar.

"We felt that the DPI Process was excellent in the sense that it was really a process that forced us to answer our own questions. And since *we* know the industry, the issues and the challenges, we felt this was the best way for us to define our own strategy, one that we would own. When it's your people's own strategy, execution becomes that much easier because they developed it, they believe in it and they have ownership of it. And it's been the same strategy since '96. We have not changed it in the slightest, even when we went through a very bad hiccup in 1998 because of a technology failure. A technology provided to us by one of our partners failed in the field. We went through a disaster, but we never took our eyes off the ball. To this day, the whole management team still feels that what kept us going was this *incredible focus* on that single sentence that DPI helped us develop called the Business Concept—*'Be the leader in wide format imaging systems and only that.'* We continue to live by that every day."

The process provided the forum that the company's management needed in order to get agreement on that concise Business Concept. In the course of the sessions it quickly became clear that the selection of a Driving Force and its related Areas of Excellence would be the platform from which their future would spring. As in most companies there were, at the beginning of the sessions, a variety of opinions among the key players as to the right Driving Force.

Says Kumar, "Some people said we should be Customer Class-driven, a one-stop solutions provider. We should offer everything a customer needs–the printer, the software, the ink, the paper. Others said, 'Let's just stay focused on one area we know well and be Technology-driven.' Still others said, 'Let's just build printers'–a Product-driven strategy. We had always talked about these three components of the business without knowing that there is a way to look at them through a concept that DPI calls 'Driving Force.' Before we went through the process and began to sort out these things," says Kumar, "we had people who would say, 'Look, we sell to this customer, why don't we develop some complementary products and sell them at the same time.' The difficulty with this concept is that when you're small, with only $25 million in business, your marketing people can only focus on so many things. They really only have the resources to focus on your own products. We began to realize, through the logic of the process, that when they go out and say to the customer, 'Let me show you some paper', or 'Let me show you some laminators,' or 'Let me show you some PCs,'–we really don't add any value from these additional activities. They don't make us any stronger in our sandbox. In fact they make us *weaker* because they dilute our limited resources. Also, we had to look at our technology, which is very good. Were we successful because we were a technology company? Or, were we successful because we understood the market the best?"

In order to fully envision the implications of each choice, the process enabled the work teams to create pictures of where each Driving Force might take the company in the future.

As Kumar explains, "We played out all three scenarios, Product, Technology and User/Customer Class. It was very clear from the moment we began these discussions that a Customer Class Driving Force, for a $25 million company trying to fulfill all the needs of a commercial printer, was not a viable strategy. We came to the same conclusion regarding the Technology-driven strategy. We had a technology that had been successful only in a very small niche area, and we couldn't see how we could expand it into other applications. The discussion that really convinced us more than anything else was that over the previous six years, we had seen exceptional growth every time we launched a new wide-format printer product. Then we'd get to a certain stage, and after a period of about six months we'd have a dry spell. We would then introduce the next product and we'd go through another dramatic surge. Everybody kind of looked at each other and said, 'Boy, this is so simple isn't it.' We are so well known as a wide-format printer *product* company. We just need to focus on the Area of Excellence called Product Development. The whole team must make sure that the product doesn't slip. We must do everything possible to nurture, support, and help the R&D Team, make them part of the strategy process, and explain how critical they are for our business and our ability to compete with the Xeroxes and the Lockheeds.

"We concluded that if we did those things we could be the *best* at Product Development. We could beat them because they move slowly, they're bigger companies, have other products to worry about and have different Driving Forces than ours. Plus, they don't have our focus. So it became clear to everyone that we should be Product-Driven. We make a specific category of wide format printers and that's it.

"Our strategy was simple, yet it gave enormous focus, and we have never deviated from that. We defined our Driving Force to be Product–'wide format printers.' We then defined our Areas of Excellence as Product Development and Sales & Service. That focus allowed us to introduce a series of new printers at a pace that the other guys could not keep up with. It was that simple concept that has set us on the path to supremacy in our sandbox."

Like the judo expert, they proceeded to use their R&D expertise and agility to move faster than their larger competitors. They began to work their Critical Issues, nurturing the Product Development Area of Excellence, and developed a stream of innovative new products, supporting them with the most knowledgeable sales and marketing force in the sandbox.

Gradually, this absolute dedication to refining and enhancing these Areas of Excellence amplified their "supremacy gap" and took its toll on their competitors. Incredibly, a couple of years later, both Xerox's and Lockheed's wide format printer divisions were *out of business* in spite of healthy growth in demand for this particular class of printer.

"I believe these competitors, because they were so much bigger first of all, couldn't focus on any one thing. Without as clear a concept as we created through the DPI Process, we overtook them in Product Development and we never faced tough competition from that day forward because their products were always from the last generation of technology. In the end, they just gave up.

"One of them, Calcomp, in our view, wasn't clear on whether they were a Product company or a Technology company. They got into developing some futuristic technology and spent a hundred million dollars on R&D, but never commercialized it. Instead of staying focused on developing printers, they developed something like an integrated circuit, a chip that goes *into* the printer. It was that lack of focus, in my mind anyway, that finally destroyed their business.

"Xerox actually pulled out of the business completely," Kumar continues. "A $200 million division is gone. Calcomp Lockheed no longer exists either; it went bankrupt. So it is really very fulfilling to see that these huge corporations with all their incredible resources and market presence, but without a focused, well articulated strategy–could fumble and just disappear," Kumar says.

Meanwhile, Raster Graphics was purchased by Gretag, a Swiss imaging company. The wide format group continues to operate autonomously and is on a rapid growth curve. But the world doesn't stand still and let a successful company like this own a profitable, growing segment unchallenged. Again, the DPI Process has provided the tools Gretag's people needed to review and revisit their sandbox, and identify potential new competitors they might encounter. This annual review has provided a basis for detecting emerging trends that might give rise to new products–and new competitors and more opportunities to enhance its supremacy of the wide format printer sandbox.

Chapter 9

The Internet:
A Strategic Weapon
Of Supremacy

"I just approved a $10 million dollar Internet project and I have absolutely no idea of what it is all about," said one of our CEO clients to us a few months ago. Unfortunately, this is a sentiment shared by many CEOs we have encountered in the last few years. They are approving large sums of money on Internet-related IT projects without a clue as to what they will be getting for their investment. In fact, last year IT expenditures accounted for close to 50% of all capital spending in the United States. The 2000th company on Fortune Magazine's Global 2000 list spends a minimum of $15 million per year on IT systems. Number 1 spends a few billion.

One of the major inconveniences, therefore, associated with the desire to join the Internet club is the need for major investments in IT systems. Unfortunately, a CEO is entering a *high stakes/high risk* arena. This is best illustrated by a study done by the Standish Group of the success or failure rates of IT projects. The results were as follows:

- 84% of all IT projects are late, over budget or canceled
- the cost to U.S. corporations last year was $184 billion
- completed projects achieve only 60% of their objectives

Why Such A High Failure Rate?

The reason is simple. Most CEOs of so-called "traditional" companies are baffled by the sudden emergence of a new variable in their universe, a variable called the Internet which no one can see, touch or feel. They don't understand the Internet and, as a result, they can't think through the implications on their business nor how to exploit it to their advantage.

Enter The Plumber

In an attempt to reduce their vulnerability to failure, or to educate themselves, they call upon a so-called Internet Expert Consultant and place their fate in the hands of this person. This is akin to making the plumber the architect of your new house. You'll end up with a lot of pipes! In business, making the external consultant the architect of your Internet strategy will result in a lot of software and hardware that satisfy the needs of the consultant's privileged suppliers rather than the needs of the company. In fact, you might even end up with a disconnect between the *business strategy* of the enterprise and the *Internet strategy.*

Our premise is that the CEO and the Executive Team must be the architects of their own Internet strategy as they are of their business strategy. This view is based on some basic *tenets* that we, at DPI, believe in deeply. These are:

- that every organization interacts with its customers in its own particular way. No two competitors do so in the same manner
- no one understands that interaction better than the company's own employees. No outside consultant can master this knowledge through "flash" visits to the company's headquarters
- that every company must develop its own "modus operandi" to use the Internet to interact with its customers. No generic systems will accomplish this.

Changing The Game Board

A successful business strategy should accommodate a constant stream of changes over time. Some changes, however, are of such magnitude that they affect the *structure,* or *genetic code,* of an enterprise and will cause every CEO to rethink the strategy and the business model that was created to deploy it.

The Internet falls in this category. The Internet will have an impact on *every product, every customer, every market, every industry and every company on this planet.*

The Internet will change the "game boards" of every industry since it puts into question many of the traditional rules of the business game:

- it disrupts the traditional value chain
- it turns assets into liabilities
- it destroys brand loyalty
- it turns value-added products into commodities
- it makes pricing transparent to both customers and competitors
- it breaks the stranglehold some companies have on captive markets
- it removes the power of pricing from the producer and places it in the hands of the customer
- it dramatically reduces transaction and switching costs
- it makes the customer much more knowledgeable and increases his/her sophistication as a buyer
- it opens up a much greater range of options for the customer
- it makes information available for "free" thus releasing long held confidential corporate trade secrets

The Ultimate e-Nigma

No change represents as important a challenge to every CEO now and in the years to come as the Internet. Because of the intangibility of the Internet, it is difficult for most executives to "get their arms around it." They can't see it, they can't touch it, and they have no experience with it or anything like it. It's an unknown and unknowns can be very unsettling. And there are good reasons for this malaise:

- There are no history books. No one has written a useful book about his or her experience with the Internet and how businesses should use it. It is a change that is happening now–in real time–and it is morphing into something different every day.
- There are no experts. In spite of their claims to the contrary, no consultants have enough experience to be considered experts yet.

They are all learning with each project, usually at the client's expense.
- There are no proven models. In spite of all the dot.com companies that have come and gone in the last few years, the fact remains that none have withstood the test of time.

Lessons From The Past

Let's go back in time to 1885-1886, when the first automobile was introduced. Who then could have foreseen the advent of concepts such as car insurance, autobahns, parking lots, drive-in restaurants, banks and theaters, and laser-read toll systems? The answer is simple: probably no one. The reason? These concepts were so foreign to most people's modus operandi that they had great difficulty adapting their thinking to accommodate them. In fact, people could hardly bring themselves to give the automobile a name. At first they called it a "horseless carriage" because it was the first carriage that did not need to be pulled by animals or humans. The best they could do was name it an "automobile," which literally means "self-moving," not a terribly mesmerizing description.

Now let's return to the present and the Internet, a concept as alien to today's executive as the horseless carriage was to the owner of the local buggy whip factory. Just as the automobile paralyzed the buggy whip factory owner from doing anything about the automobile because of its "alienness," the Internet is paralyzing today's CEO. To overcome this paralysis, management needs to "get their arms around it."

Demystifying The e-Nigma

The Internet is a mystery to most executives, and any mystery is a challenge to a good problem-solver. Since we at DPI consider ourselves problem-solvers, some time ago we embarked on a journey to crack the enigma and make it understandable to lay people.

The e-Nablers™

The Internet e-nigma can be demystified only if one understands the Internet's capabilities and can rationally identify where, when and how the Internet will affect one's business model. We have found that the Internet has 12 basic capabilities, or e-nablers^{TM}, that can impact any business:

* Aggregation   * Marketable knowledge

* Build-to-order   * Product re-bundling

* Customer self-service   * Market exchanges

* Producer direct   * Dynamic pricing

* Channel integration   * Portals

* Syndication   * 1:1 Marketing

Aggregation

Aggregation is the capability of recruiting large groups of buyers and/or sellers in order to obtain better costs or prices. The Internet facilitates two forms of aggregation: demand aggregation and supply aggregation. This is a key capability of the Internet which enables an organization to aggregate demand for a certain product or service and then use that volume to obtain better prices. A good example is priceline.com which originated the use of this e-nabler. The day that priceline.com went on-line, it removed the airlines' control over their ability to price their product and placed it in the hands of consumers.

Priceline assembles large numbers of people who want to travel by air and then uses this accumulated volume to exert pressure on airlines to come up with the cheapest price. Over 200,000 people per week were using this service at its peak prior to the problems the company encountered by extending itself into other areas too quickly.

Two current examples of *supply* aggregators are Wal-Mart and Home Depot. These two companies do the opposite of Priceline. Instead of recruiting large numbers of consumers–demand–they recruit large numbers of vendors–supply–and extract the lowest cost and pass on the savings to their customers.

Build-To-Order

No company is better suited to find an Internet e-nabler that directly supports its business strategy than Dell Computer. The "build-to-order" e-nabler was "made-to-order" for Dell. As its name implies, the "build-to-order" e-nabler does exactly that…it allows customers to place orders for products configured to each customer's specific requirements. In fact, Dell should not be referred to as a "computer manufacturer" but rather as a "computer configurator" which is a better description of its business strategy.

Customer Self Service

FedEx Custom Critical, a DPI client, discovered this e-nabler during their use of our e-Strategy Process which is described in a later chapter.

The company's business strategy is based on exploiting breakdowns in the Just-In-Time delivery system in place between companies and their suppliers everywhere these exist. Whenever this system fails and the goods needed do not arrive on time, FedEx Custom Critical's strategy kicks in, and the company receives a call from a customer who finds himself in that predicament. As mentioned earlier, FedEx Custom Critical has two thousand trucks strategically located around the country waiting for such a call. While on the phone with a dispatcher, and using a sophisticated satellite system, the customer is guaranteed a specific time when the item will be picked up and delivered.

When FedEx management was introduced to the Customer Self Service e-nabler they suddenly discovered that, instead of going through a dispatcher, the customer could be given direct access to its fleet of trucks. Using the satellite system, the customer could locate the closest truck to the supplier's facility, and contract with the truck operator directly, thus bypassing the dispatcher altogether.

This is exploiting an Internet e-nabler called Customer Self Service, and it put further distance between them and their competitors, greatly enhancing their supremacy in their sandbox.

Producer Direct

No one group of people is as concerned about the Internet, probably, as Insurance Agents. And justifiably so! At the root of their concern is an e-nabler called *producer direct.* The Internet provides a producer, or manufacturer of a product or service, with the opportunity to sell directly to the end user, thus bypassing the traditional methods of selling and distributing through third party agents, reps or distributors.

This e-nabler is a death threat to all intermediaries between a producer and a customer. This is called disintermediation and is particularly prevalent in the area of intangible services such as insurance. Many CEOs of insurance companies are currently agonizing over this very issue and it is of strategic importance to the future of these firms.

Channel Integration

This e-nabler is the exact opposite of the one just discussed. Instead of disintermediating the existing channels, this e-nabler attempts to integrate them, using the Internet, into a coherent sales and distribution system that gives the company an additional competitive advantage.

Two companies currently deploying this e-nabler are Home Depot and The Gap. Home Depot has integrated the Internet with its stores and catalog. A customer can browse through the Home Depot catalog, select an item, order and pay for it on-line, and pick it up at the local store at a pre-arranged time. The Gap uses this e-nabler in a similar manner by integrating its catalog, stores and advertising through the Internet. The whole system is also seamless. A customer can buy on the Internet, take delivery through the Postal Service or UPS, discover the item does not fit and return it to any store for a full credit.

Channel Integration might be the e-nabler to solve the "broker dilemma" faced by insurance company CEOs mentioned before. Some forms of insurance which are self-explanatory, such as term insurance, can probably be sold over the Internet, while more complex forms which require consultation with an expert could continue to be handled through brokers and agents.

Syndication

Syndication enables a company to sell products or services to customers who then "package" these with other products that have been "syndicated" from other suppliers whom, in turn, resell or deliver the "package" to a third party.

Syndication, now available through the Internet, brings together three players, each with a different role. The first is the originator, an organization that creates the content, such as Disney with its continuous flow of animated film characters. Others are Charles Schulz and Scott Adams, the "originators" of Charlie Brown and Dilbert, respectively.

The second player in this drama is the syndicator, the organization that buys the originator's content, combines it with content from other originators and packages this content in a variety of formats to attract the third party in this play - the distributor. An example is a company called United Features which purchases Schulz's and Adams' comic strips, packages these with others and sells these to newspaper companies all over the world.

The distributor is the organization which interacts with customers. The distributor uses syndication as a method to reduce the cost of acquiring content. E-Trade is a good example of a distributor.

E-Trade syndicates content from Reuters for news; Bridge Information for quotes; Big Charts for stock price graphics, etc. The Internet accelerates the flow of information, and thus the syndication of products by .com companies.

Marketable Knowledge

Over the course of time, every organization accumulates large volumes of knowledge that relates to various parts of its business. In many instances, that knowledge is stored and left to rot. The Internet provides a capability that enables a company to turn idle knowledge into a valuable asset by digitizing it and making it available on the Web.

One of our clients is Cancer Treatment Centers of America (CTCA). Its CEO, Dick Stephenson, is on a crusade to eradicate cancer from this planet. Over the years, CTCA has accumulated vast quantities of information about various aspects of cancer that, until recently, lay dormant in one or the other of its several facilities. Much of that information would be of great interest to new cancer patients to help educate themselves about their disease. Medical professionals, such as doctors in training, would also be interested in having access to this data.

This year, CTCA has done just that. It has created a web site that is organized by cancer category and makes available, for free, all the treatment options, both traditional and holistic, in order to help patients make more informed decisions.

Every organization has a bank of experiential data that could be "packaged" in a variety of different forms, to be sold on the Internet, creating brand new revenue streams for the organization.

Product Re-bundling

Cendant Corporation is a conglomerate that owns several hotel chains, car rental companies, travel agency chains and a real estate franchiser named Century 21. Until recently, these all were operated as separate businesses although it was always the CEO's strategy to combine their product offerings in some manner. Unfortunately, he did not have a mechanism to make that occur and the synergy that he was seeking did not materialize…that is …until the Internet arrived.

This e-nabler, called product re-bundling, allows an entity to use the Internet to bundle closely related, but separate and different, products or services, in combinations that could not occur on a stand-alone basis. The new e-commerce entity prospers by adding value in a manner that the separate organizations cannot.

A good friend of ours is in the process of setting up an Internet company whose strategy is totally based on exploiting this e-nabler. The concept is brilliant. The company has negotiated agreements with the major universities and book publishers for the right to reproduce digitally all of their "knowledge" manuscripts. The company will then resell the content of these publications, in whole or in part, which will then be downloaded from the Internet. In fact, you will be able to order Chapters 2 & 6 from one book located in one library and Chapters 3 & 8 from another book in a different library and, fifteen minutes later pick it up, nicely bound, at your local Kinko's.

Market Exchanges

This e-nabler is the opposite of the first one we discussed called Demand Aggregation. In this case, producers aggregate production volumes in a given industry so that customers can easily find out how much and where product is available. In some industries, the market exchange e-nabler allows interested customers to bid on the inventory that is available.

Two current examples of this e-nabler at work are plasticsnet.com and metalsite.com. Both are sponsored by several producers in that industry which publish their inventory and then hold on-line auctions.

These exchanges provide a more cost efficient method to get products to markets. Market Exchanges exist in many industries and are probably the most popular of all twelve e-nablers.

Dynamic Pricing

This e-nabler takes Market Exchanges one step further. As the word "dynamic" implies, products offered through this e-nabler come with "dynamic," possibly even "volatile," prices. Like the classic law of "supply and demand," the price varies with each transaction depending on the balance between demand and supply. Sometimes the producer wins; sometimes the customer wins.

One company that is currently testing this e-nabler is Budget Rent-a-Car. This innovative company allows customers to make an offer as to what he/she is willing to pay depending on how many cars are on the lot at any one time of the day. Budget then accepts or rejects that offer based on this number. As a result, the price is "dynamic" in that the price can be different with every transaction.

Portals

A portal is a web capability developed by an organization upon which the company offers its own products as well as products from competitors. The company does this to be perceived as an "objective" party to the buying process. It then hopes that this "objectivity" will bring them their fair share of the sales generated.

One example of a company using this e-nabler is the insurance company discussed earlier called Progressive. Its web site is a "portal" for its own insurance products as well as for some of its competitors. Progressive gladly "refers" prospects to its lower priced competitors because its proprietary software is designed to weed out potentially unprofitable customers up front.

1:1 Marketing

The other day, while reading my favorite weekly sports magazine, I turned to page 67 to discover the following message:

> "Michel Robert
> Are you considering refinancing your home
> mortgage? If you are, please call us for a
> better rate.
>
> ABC Bank"

So surprised was I by seeing my name printed on page 67 that I read the rest of the advertisement, something I never do. This is called 1:1 Marketing. Electronic technology allows companies to construct data bases that can store enormous amounts of information which can be used to zero-in on a prospect with a clearly defined profile, one-on-one. The Internet allows this to happen on your PC rather than in a magazine. This technique is called narrowcasting as opposed to broadcasting, which is targeted at a broad audience, and will be the marketing method of choice in the future.

The e-Nabler: Unleashing Internet Innovation

Once your people understand these twelve e-nablers, they can now think of many ways where these capabilities can be exploited across the business. The issue now is to ensure that these Internet e-nablers are deployed in a manner that supports the business strategy of the enterprise and contributes to enhancing your supremacy over your competitors.

Mark O'Brien

President & Chief Operating Officer

Framing An e-Strategy

It may be possible to build a house without a blueprint, especially for an experienced builder if he has built a similar structure before. He knows what it will look like, what materials to use, what it's likely to cost, and what kinds of problems he may run into. While it can be done, it's certainly not the most intelligent way to build a house. Unfortunately a lot of companies have tried to do the same thing with their Internet initiatives with disastrous results–cost overruns, overlapping applications and projects that seem to go on endlessly. The fundamental differences between the house and the Internet are that there are no proven Internet models for the business. No one's ever built one like it before. No one knows what it should "look like," how long it will take, what problems will be encountered, what it will cost–and most importantly whether it will do what's needed to support the business strategy.

Pulte Corporation had been quite involved in the Internet over the past three-plus years, implementing a reasonably well-developed plan. Yet early in 2000, the people at Pulte–a major national homebuilder that *does* use blueprints to build their houses–saw that the time had come to design a comprehensive blueprint for an Internet strategy that would fully support their *business* strategy. They elected to use DPI's e-Strategy Process to do it. But let's step back a bit in time to see how they arrived at that conclusion.

Building The Business Strategy

In the mid 90's, Pulte Corporation set out to "change the rules of play in the home building market," as CEO Bob Burgess then stated. Through DPI's Strategic Thinking Process, the then $2 billion company committed to several ambitious goals–including doubling the size of the company by the year 2000, which it has successfully accomplished.

The guiding mantra through the ensuing years of extraordinary growth has always been "delight the customer." Most people who have been through the process of building a home know that the experience can be fraught with delays, blown budgets and disappearing contractors. It can be anything but delightful. Pulte was determined to change all that.

First, they trimmed down the company by shedding businesses unrelated to home building. Pulte got down to a solid foundation–its homebuilding and home mortgage businesses. Then it worked to apply more sophisticated marketing techniques for understanding its customers and markets and focused on delivering the highest quality home possible. This work evolved into a strategy Pulte calls Homeowner For Life™, which seeks to extend the strong customer relationship Pulte develops over the course of building a customer's new home. The ultimate goal of Homeowner for Life™ is to sell additional products and services by maintaining that customer relationship long after the house sale is complete.

These concepts required the integration of skills not always found in home building–market research, consumer marketing and an obsession with quality improvement throughout its complex value chain and sales process. Pulte's exceptional growth in sales and profits as well as consistently high customer satisfaction marks attest to the success of its strategy.

Enter The Internet

In the midst of all this change, Pulte, as early as 1995, had recognized the emergence of technology as an important tool to improve and grow the business. Its embrace of technology was ahead of many companies in the homebuilding industry. This trend continued as Pulte was an early adopter in using the Internet to support its business operations. As technology and the Internet became an increasingly important part of the business, they felt the need for a cohesive overall strategy and opted for DPI's e-Strategy Process to help them create it.

As President and COO Mark O'Brien recalls, "We began to develop a long-range e-business plan that would help guide us for the foreseeable future. As part of this process, we formed an e-business team to develop a more comprehensive Internet strategy. The preliminary work of this group provided a pretty solid foundation that we brought into the DPI Process. The DPI Process helped us define and validate the strategy and prioritize some of the underlying tactics. That's the junction in the road we found ourselves in. Seven or eight years ago, Mike Robert and the DPI team assisted us in developing a strategic plan. That experience was positive and we thought Mike could provide some of the same assistance in developing our e-Strategy. By coincidence, DPI had just developed a process to help companies formulate an e-Strategy.

"Pulte had already developed a number of e-Business initiatives focused on capturing B-to-C and B-to-B business opportunities. We had established an e-Business team reporting directly to senior management, guiding and implementing our process. We really saw the DPI Process as a tool to help us focus and prioritize our Internet related activities that are designed to support Pulte's core home building business."

People from a wide array of disciplines within Pulte were assembled to hammer out their new e-Strategy. One of the most critical steps in the process is to bring the group to a common understanding of the Internet's potential effects. To accomplish this, DPI has developed a set of twelve *e-nablers*™ , which represent the Internet's basic business models. These e-nablers demystify the Internet for business people by identifying specific capabilities of the Internet that can be used to leverage a company's key strengths.

"Understanding of the Internet varied widely," says O'Brien. "We assembled a group of about sixty people to go through this process. Some had great knowledge of the Internet and e-Business, while others are more focused on our traditional homebuilding activities and thus less exposed and conversant with the powers of e-Commerce.

"The e-nabler framework is a great way to present a complex series of concepts. I know the participants in our group who were unfamiliar with Internet-based business models found the information helped focus their thoughts and ideas as we advanced through the subsequent stages of the DPI Process."

Once the e-nablers were understood, the core business and information processes that tie the company together were then mapped in detail. The Process allowed the work teams to identify the Points of Impact where these different e-nablers may affect these processes, positively and negatively.

A list of specific potential Internet applications was then developed that would leverage the positive impacts and mitigate the negative ones. These applications were then filtered for strategic fit, cost, benefits, and ease of implementation. The resulting short list was deemed to be the applications most crucial to supporting the business strategy.

As O'Brien comments, "One of the interesting results having gone through the e-Strategy Process was that each of the teams came up with applications working independently which had a lot of common characteristics. There were several overlaps and links between one another. As we developed our Internet blueprint, we were able to merge all of our various disciplines and visions into a real value chain of e-Commerce.

"We are in the very final stages of a comprehensive Internet blueprint that will address all aspects of our home building value chain from managing the customer experience to efficiently linking our contractors, vendors and suppliers. We're now working to set priorities and establish the teams that will drive the implementation as we go forward.

"I don't think there's any question but that as a result of going through the e-Strategy Process we eliminated some applications from our previously articulated strategy, added some others, and, in fact, identified a lot of enhancements that will have value. Fully implementing this program will take place over a period of months and maybe years, but at least we're beginning with the end in mind.

"Having gone through the Strategic Thinking Process seven years ago and arriving at a clear strategic direction for the company, and now exploiting the e-nablers together with our strengths and understanding the competitive environment that we were in, there is every reason to believe that we will get the same positive result from our e-Business strategy that we got for our corporate strategy."

A Look at e-Competition

The Process then gave Pulte the opportunity to look at the Internet from their competitors' perspective. The "Competitor.com" Team used the process to determine how competitors might use the Internet.

"The Competitor Team did a great job of providing insight into where the industry is likely to head, and how specific competitors might respond to our various initiatives at Pulte. Working independently from the rest of the teams, I think the Competitor Team validated many of the strategic initiatives that we are considering, while at the same time highlighting some of the opportunities and risks inherent in our approach. Overall I think it was a very valuable contributor to the process and a necessary one," O'Brien states.

In a similar vein, the "Killer.com" Team was given the assignment of designing a new e-Competitor whose purpose would be to invalidate Pulte's business model and possibly put Pulte out of business. What form would it take? How vulnerable would Pulte be? What can the company do now to mitigate such a threat?

Though he understandably provides no specifics, O'Brien says simply, "With respect to the Killer.com Team, they did some very interesting work. I think as the result of their work, we are incorporating some features into our strategy that will insulate us from The Killer. We have a vision of that Killer.com, but I don't think we got absolute clarity because that Killer may manifest itself in varying ways over the years to come. But I think we have an idea where it would come from and what we might do about it."

Indeed, the flexibility of both DPI's Strategic Thinking Process and e-Strategy Process may be what gives these processes strength and longevity within an organization. As they become part of the fabric of the company's thinking, they provide a basis for continuous re-evaluation as the world changes. This is particularly crucial with the Internet, since the future is filled with unknown developments.

Says O'Brien, "On the other hand, I think there are some knowns. The Internet has touched every one of us. It is changing the way we live on a daily basis. I don't think there is any question but that it is changing the home building landscape, as it is many other businesses. I think we just need to be prepared to develop with it. We're obviously excited about the future. I think the Process we've been through added clarity to our e-Business strategy. As we go forward, we will continue to apply many of the tools that are in the DPI kit to varying opportunities that the e-Commerce world presents to us."

Perhaps the most important result is that Pulte now has an agreed-upon e-Strategy that fully supports its business strategy, which has proven to be successful throughout the last decade.

"Our vision is to effectively link the entire home building value chain from customers to contractors and suppliers," O'Brien states. "We recognize that this is an ambitious undertaking. It will require an enormous investment of people and financial resources. The DPI Process helped us be more specific and precise about the potential benefits associated with these various programs, as well as how best to prioritize the initiatives.

"Pulte Corporation is a homebuilder. We will continue to focus on our core home building business, delighting our customers with every house we build and the entire home buying, building and ownership experience. e-Business is not a separate activity. It needs to add value, must add value in fact, and be integrated into our day-to-day operations and support our core home building and mortgage businesses. It's the function of technology to support and enhance communications with our customers and our business partners before, during and after the home is built. And I think the DPI Process helps ensure that we will retain that focus."

Chapter 10

Create Products That Breed Strategic Supremacy

There was a time, not so long ago, when one could walk into any office anywhere in the world and see hundreds of Friden calculators on row upon row of wooden desks.

There was a time, not so long ago, when one could walk into any office anywhere in the world and see dozens of duplicating machines made by Addressograph Multigraph.

There was a time, not so long ago, when one could walk into any store, large or small, anywhere in the world and see one cash register, if not several, made by the National Cash Register Company (NCR).

There was a time, not so long ago, when one could go into any house in the United States, and some one hundred other countries, and find a Singer sewing machine.

There was a time, not so long ago, when these four companies–Singer, Addressograph Multigraph, NCR and Friden–were industrial powerhouses who had worldwide supremacy over all their competitors. However, just a few years later, their supremacy has disintegrated and these companies are on the verge of extinction.

What did these companies do, or not do, to go from the ecstasy of supremacy to the footnotes of corporate history books?

Lack Of Strategic Product Innovation

The strategy of a company is deployed through the introduction and commercialization of new products. Therefore, any company that wishes to perpetuate its supremacy over a long period of time, needs to have in place an on-going and aggressive *new product development program.* Unfortunately, such was not the case in the four companies mentioned above. Many other companies, which had on-going new product development programs, could extend their supremacy over their competitors for very long periods of time, companies such as Johnson & Johnson, Merck, Mercedes, Sony, Honda ...to name but a few. Recognizing this phenomenon, we then set out to codify the *process* that creates products that breed strategic supremacy over time.

New Products Are Not Always New Products

As noted in a previous chapter, the "profile" of a company is seen in the nature of the products the company offers, the nature of customers it makes these available to, the nature of the market segments that these customers reside in and the nature of the geographic markets it operates in.

If a CEO wishes to change the *profile* of the company, this is done by the creation and commercialization of *new* products. During our research into the subject of product innovation, we noticed that most companies concentrate their entire product innovation effort on incremental or marginal improvements to *existing products.* This type of product innovation is not strategic in nature since there is no attempt to change the "look" of the products the company offers.

In fact, while working with companies considered the best at product innovation, we discovered that even these companies had difficulty defining what a *new product* was. Thus our first area of investigation was to identify the various categories of new product opportunities. Over time, we uncovered *five* categories of new product opportunities. These are:

New-to-the-market. These are products that, when introduced, were unique to the market and the world. No similar products existed anywhere. Examples consist of 3M's Post-it® Notes, Sony's Walkman and its VCR.

New-to-Us. When Panasonic introduced its own version of the VCR, it was not new-to-the-market since Sony had done it before, but it was new to Panasonic.

Product Extensions. In this category, we find two types: *Incremental and Quantum Leap*. An example of an incremental extension is 3M's adaptation of the original Post-it Notes into larger sizes, shapes and colors. Airbus' announcement that it will produce an airplane that will carry 800 people instead of 300 is an example of a quantum leap extension. It will require a lot more ingenuity to keep 800 people up there than 300.

New Customers. This category applies to the introduction of current products to current customers.

New Markets. This category applies to the introduction of current products to new market segments or new geographic areas.

The Em-phá-sis On The Wrong Syl-lá-ble

The next area we investigated was: In which category did they invest most of their resources? Guess what over 200 companies answered. Right! *Product extensions*…of the *incremental* type. Unfortunately, incremental extensions only bring *incremental revenues*. Only *new-to-the-market* products create new revenue streams. Most companies are putting their em-phá-sis on the wrong syl-lá-ble. In other words, they are pouring their money into the wrong type of product innovation.

The Four Deadly Sins That Kill Strategic Product Innovation

Since new-to-the-market products are the essence of strategic supremacy, we then set out to identify the obstacles that caused companies to spend almost all of their time, money and energy on product extensions at the expense of new-to-the-market products. Our discovery? Most companies practiced one, or more, of four habits that killed new product creation and led to a company's loss of supremacy over its competitors. Unfortunately, all four were self-inflicted wounds.

Too Much Focus On Current Customers

What person do most books on product innovation tell you to consult in order to get inspiration for new products? The obvious answer: your customers. Wrong ...dead wrong! If a company focuses its entire effort on current customers as a source for new products, it will always end up with *incremental* products. The reason is very simple. *Current* customers are very good at telling you what is *currently wrong* with your *current product*. They can do this well because they do side-by-side comparisons and they identify *performance gaps* in your product relative to your competitors. Naturally, you go back to the factory, tweak the product a little, and come back with an incremental improvement. And the pattern is set and keeps repeating itself. What current customers are not very competent at is telling you what they will need *in the future.* Some examples.

Not one of 3M's millions of customers ever asked 3M for Post-it Notes. Not one of Chrysler's millions of customers ever asked for a minivan. Not one of Sony's millions of customers ever asked Mr.Morita for a Walkman or a VCR. No one on this planet ever asked Steve Jobs and Steve Wozniak for an Apple PC. And the list goes on. These are all products which originated in the minds of the *creator not the recipient.* There is a very good reason for this as articulated by Akio Morita, the founder of Sony:

> "Our plan is to influence the public with new
> products instead of asking which products
> they want. The public doesn't know what is
> possible. We do."

Another person who said it as eloquently was the recently retired CEO of 3M, Livio DeSimone:

> "The most interesting products are the ones
> that people need but can't articulate that
> they need."

In order to breed strategic supremacy and create *new revenue streams,* therefore, it is imperative to concentrate a company's product innovation resources on *new-to-the-market* products. These are products that satisfy *future implicit needs* that you have identified and that your customers cannot articulate to you today. In this manner, the result will be products that will allow you to *change the game and perpetuate your supremacy.* The DPI process described in a later chapter was designed to do exactly that.

Protect The "Cash Cow" Mentality

Every company, over time, has products that become cash cows. *Never worship at the altar of the cash cow.* You will lose your supremacy. IBM is a case in point.

IBM's cash cow, as we all know, has been its mainframes–once the workhorses of the computing industry. In 1968, in its Swiss laboratories, IBM invented the first microchip–the RISC chip–with more processing capacity than its smaller mainframes. A small computer prototype, powered by this chip, was built and could have been the first PC the world would have seen. IBM, however, made a deliberate decision *not* to introduce that chip because it could foresee the devastation it might have on its mainframe business. In 1994, 26 years later and maybe 26 years too late, IBM finally introduced the RISC chip under the name PowerPC. In the meantime, IBM lost the opportunity to be the powerhouse in the *consumer* market that it is in the *business* market.

The Mature Market Syndrome

"Our industry is mature. There is no more growth in these markets."

Many would claim that the reason products become generic, prices come down to the lowest levels, and growth stops is that the "market is mature." Mature markets, in our view, are a myth.

Consider some examples. Who would have thought 15 years ago that people would pay $300 for a pair of shoes? Running shoes at that! After all, everyone had a pair of $5 sneakers and the market was mature. Then along came Nike and Reebok and the "mature market" exploded.

Who would have thought 15 years ago that people would pay $4000 for a bicycle? After all, everyone had a $50 bicycle and the market was mature.

Then along came Shimano with its 10, 20, 25 speed bicycles and the "mature market" exploded.

Two CEOs who have based their success on the notion of "mature" markets are Jack Welch of General Electric and Lawrence Bossidy, formerly CEO of Allied Signal. Jack Welch preaches that "mature markets are a state of mind" while Bossidy says that "there is no such thing as a mature market. What we need are *mature executives* who can make markets grow."

The Commodity Product Fallacy

"We're in the commodity business" is another mindset that can bring down a company's supremacy. This is also a state of mind. Products become commodities when management *convinces* itself that they are. It's a self-fulfilling prophecy.

An example is baking soda, a "commodity" product that has been around since the days of the Pharaohs. Until someone placed a small quantity in a refrigerator and noticed that it absorbed odors. Not so long after, we had baking soda deodorant. Then came baking soda toothpaste and recently, baking soda diapers.

Then there is the "mother" of all commodities–water. Yet, look at what the French can do with water. They have mastered the marketing of this mundane commodity by branding it under a variety of names such as Vitel, Evian and Perrier. They charge you "x" for a bottle of plain water. They then add bubbles and charge you "2x". They then add cherry flavoring and charge you "3x". Cherry and raspberry will cost you "4x" and the game, in which they reign supreme, goes on.

New-to-the-Market Products Breed Supremacy

Sony, 3M, Rubbermaid, Canon, Microsoft, Johnson & Johnson, Caterpillar, Hewlett Packard, Schwab and many others control the sandbox, not by introducing "me-too" products but, rather, by focusing its resources on the creation of new-to-the-market products which have three inherent characteristics that contribute to breeding supremacy over their competitors:

- A period of *exclusivity.* When you are the only product in the market, you are the *only one*
- During this period of exclusivity, you can obtain *premium prices* as opposed to me-too products where every transaction comes down to haggling over price
- Being first to the market allows you to build in barriers that make it very difficult for competitors to gain entry into your game

After all, that's what supremacy is all about: changing the game and creating the rules that competitors who wish to play your game must submit to.

William S. Rafferty

Senior Vice President

Best Product Wins

"If all you do is mimic your competitor's tactics, and if *they're* thinking clearly about *their* competitive advantages," says Bill Rafferty of Mestek, Inc., "you're spending all of your resources doing what *they're* better at. How many times have you seen that–companies chasing their competitors when that's exactly the wrong thing to do?"

Rafferty is a Senior Vice President at Mestek, a Massachusetts-based company with over twenty-five divisions that make a variety of equipment primarily for the HVAC and metal-forming markets. Among his responsibilities, he oversees Mestek's Boiler business unit, a three-unit division that in 2000 had reached something of an impasse in a market full of "me-too" competitors. At the time, he was in search of a new strategy to break the logjam.

"You could call us a mini-conglomerate of many businesses, with a bias towards two markets," Rafferty says of Mestek. "Our sales are about $300 million in HVAC and about $100 million in metal forming equipment. We have multiple divisions with mutually supportive franchises and channels of distribution. In most cases, we have been able to achieve a number one or number two market share in generally smaller-type niche markets where we're big fish in a lot of small ponds."

Through the 1990s, Mestek had acquired a number of companies–Westcast, RBI and Hydrotherm–that make a variety of commercial and residential boilers and water heaters. By early 2000 all three companies were prospering to varying degrees, with RBI growing at around 50% each year. Yet Westcast and Hydrotherm were still not performing to the levels that Rafferty believed they could. Despite having the backing of a substantial parent, these two units continued to play the game all of its rivals played–mimicking the market leader's product offerings and marketing tactics...a difficult game to win. The time was ripe to develop a new strategy to accelerate growth and pull away from their competitors.

"About a year ago, while I was very satisfied with the progress at RBI, I felt we were 'stuck in neutral' with the progress at the Hydrotherm and Westcast franchises. While they had achieved a certain level of success, I was searching for a 'breakout' strategy to go significantly beyond that and needed some help in thinking that through," Rafferty recalls.

"And let me tell you why 'breaking out' is particularly difficult in our industry. We have manufacturers reps that sell our products, generally to plumbing and heating wholesalers who in turn sell the products to installing contractors. Many of those products are often specified by consulting engineers. So you have multiple, interdependent buying influences with brand preferences, and a 'mature' industry with entrenched competitors. It is very difficult to significantly change the paradigm without addressing all of the buying influences simultaneously. So it's traditionally been a battle on all fronts. We knew it would be slow going, unless we could find a different way to accelerate our progress."

Coincidentally, Rafferty was involved in a DPI Strategic Thinking session at another Mestek subsidiary and was impressed by the process. He decided to take the Boiler Group's key management through DPI's process.

"I have been involved with strategic planning since early on in my career, and have tried to read and study much on the matter," he explains. "And most practitioners in this field take you through an analysis where you identify each competitor's strengths and weaknesses, you look for your high ground and then you develop a strategy based on that. The DPI Process takes you to that point but what it then does, is to suggest a way of *changing the competitive landscape.*

"DPI has advanced the concept that you can make your *competitors irrelevant.* And I would share that view with the caveat that I would say in our case, *much less* relevant. The process allows you to develop a vision and a strategy *that truly puts you in greater control of your own destiny,* and really allows you to spend much more time thinking about where *you* want to go, rather than what the *competition* is doing."

"The whole concept of the Driving Force was new to us," Rafferty says. "But we quickly discovered we were Product Driven–Boilers and Water Heaters. We learned the concept of what a Product Driven company really needs to excel at, and that is both Product Development, and Sales and Customer Support. That helped define, with DPI's help, the Critical Issues that we need to address.

"One of the more interesting things that came out of it was a better understanding of *what not to do,* which is probably more important than *what to do.* What you can see as you go through the process is that you can be easily seduced into trying to do everything, and be all things to all people, and do everything your competitors do. To a certain extent I think we had been guilty of this.

"So to help us avoid falling into that, the process allowed us to crystallize our direction through the Strategic Filter concept. That really gave our management team an aid in decision-making they can use every day to decide what to do, and more importantly, what *not* to do. That has been a very good concept for us, and has helped us to stay focused."

At the top of the "more emphasis" list, of course, was an all-out commitment to developing an on-going string of unique, new-to-the-market products that would clearly differentiate Mestek from the competition. Not necessarily "Big Bang" types of products, but equipment carefully engineered to provide significant advantages that would appeal to product specifiers. The flip side, the "what not to do", is a de-emphasis of "me-too" products, a task which requires a discipline as rigorous as creating new products.

"I would say that the product lines that we have been developing as a result of these decisions are unique. In our business it will be 'he who has the best *product* and distribution wins.' So we're *very much* de-emphasizing 'me-too' products. Now I will tell you that there is still a certain amount of inertia, a feeling that–our competition has that, we need it as well. And it is a discipline that we need to adhere to, to say at the end of the day–what does it do for us to have that 'me-too' product? While some of them need to be in the line, they're clearly not our focus. So our emphasis on which type of products to develop and nurture has clearly changed. That has actually led to us deciding to discontinue certain product lines over time. Two will be discontinued this year. That's not to say that all these products that are de-emphasized will be discontinued but some will, and the others will get less of our product development resources," says Rafferty.

The challenge has then been to determine specific characteristics that would, in combination, create products that offer differentiating advantages over competitive products–no small order in an industry where no huge technological leaps are emerging.

"In an industry as mature as ours, I don't think we anticipate major changes in the basic technologies or the competitive landscape. While the basic technology doesn't change much, the way you *apply* the technology can. *And that's where the new products stem from,*" Rafferty explains.

To assure that all this product development results in the increased profitability they were looking for in the first place, a heightened focus has been placed on the financial expectations from this push, and how to effectively bring these new products to market.

As Rafferty says, "Mike Robert asked us to first define our financial goals. And I told him that if we could achieve revenue growth of 15% a year and have a return on our investments of at least 30%–pre-tax, pre-interest–we would feel that we were being reasonably successful. Mike then challenged us to specifically put a plan together, within the Boiler Group, to achieve those objectives. And this had to be backed up with very specific targets, very specific product lines, and so forth. It's in effect saying that if you want to achieve these goals, show me how you're going to do it! So that was very good. We could look at these objectives and say, can we really achieve this or are we kidding ourselves? In our case, the critical issue now to achieving these results is the introduction of new products, *now*, that create new revenue streams. If there's anything we knew, but that hit us over the head through the DPI Process, it was that new product development is *absolutely critical* to our success. And by developing products that are different, unique, and specifiable, we do make our competition less relevant. In that regard, we are in charge of our own destiny because we create new products that set us apart.

"So we have a stream of products under development. My greatest concern is, are we improving our effectiveness in bringing these products to market as quickly as possible? We're implementing new product development procedures on our highest priority projects. We clearly understand the objectives and financial implications of the project. We have formed cross-functional teams that have clear ownership of the project. And they are asked to update the Boiler Group's management monthly on how the project is proceeding–Are they on schedule? Are the financials still looking as projected? The new procedures also force marketing to be a lot more specific about the product specifications before going into a project. You know often times you can have a 'creative creep' where the objectives are a moving target as you get into product development. We're trying to provide much more discipline to that, which we hope will hasten our introduction of these new products."

The other Area of Excellence critical to the Boiler Group's Product-driven strategy is Sales and Customer Support. Mestek made an early commitment to the Internet to improve Sales and Customer Support, largely driven by Rafferty and a couple of other people.

To bring more of the organization into the latest thinking on the importance of the Internet, DPI came back to facilitate its e-Strategy Process.

"This process helped us identify a number of new Internet applications that will further help us seek supremacy of our sandbox. The demystification of the Internet through DPI's twelve e-nablers together with their concept of a 'stealth' competitor brought us two very different ways of looking at our strategy and helped us explore strategy options that we would not have considered otherwise," he says.

As for the overall strategy of the Boiler Group, it is still too early to see the hard results. But Rafferty is optimistic that the strategy will produce the results they seek.

"We went through the DPI Process in July," says Rafferty. "Everyone left feeling very excited that we now had a breakout strategy, that we had a way of making the competition much less relevant. It helped us a great deal in developing our Business Plan for 2001 and beyond. We have a stream of new products that we're working very hard to introduce. That should begin by the middle of this year and continue through next year. These products have outstanding financial as well as strategic opportunities.

"In addition, we continue now to scour everywhere to learn how we can be better at product development. We're in discussions with lots of different types of people about the various tools and methods they have, so that we can become as effective as possible."

For CEOs considering using Strategic Thinking, Rafferty offers this observation: "At the end of the Process you can expect that all of your management team will share a vision and a Strategic Filter set, so decisions can be made daily at all levels that are consistent with the strategy. The shared *clarity and focus of what to do and what not to do*, are among the biggest benefits."

For Mestek it holds the promise of stepping ahead of a game that's been played the same way by the same rules for as long as anyone can remember.

Chapter 11

Process, Content
And The Role Of The CEO

In every strategy session that we facilitate, there are always two dynamics at work, namely *process* and *content*. Content is information or knowledge that is company or industry specific. Telephone company executives know a lot about cables, switch gears, PBX's, analog or digital devices, transmission, etc. They know all this "content" because they were "brought up" in the industry and that is the content that is specific to that industry. It is piece and parcel of their lexicon.

Executives at 3M or Caterpillar, however, know nothing about analog or digital devices or switch gears but they do know a lot about their own "content." At 3M, all executives at the top have degrees in chemistry or chemical engineering and, as a result, can talk for hours about polymer chemistry and its use in coating and abrasive applications. Such is their world.

At Caterpillar, executives can mesmerize you for hours talking about metallurgy, welding, payloads, diesel horsepower and their ability to "cut iron" better than anyone else. This is their "content" and …their comfort zone.

In order to climb up the ladder in most companies one needs to be a "content expert." This is necessary in order to be able to manage your way through the day-to-day "content laden" operational issues. Most executives get to the top of their respective silos because of their content expertise.

At the strategic level, which is above the silos, content expertise alone is not sufficient. In fact, too much content knowledge may be a major impediment to good strategic thinking. This is because strategic thinking is *process-based* rather than *content-based*. Operational management requires the skill of *analysis* while strategic management requires the skill of *synthesis*.

Analysis is the ability to study content and put it into logical *quantitative* pieces. Synthesis is the ability to make rational decisions based on highly subjective, sometimes ambiguous or incomplete pieces of data. Synthesis is highly *qualitative* in nature. Strategic thinking falls in this category. It is the ability to take subjective data and opinions and bring these into an *objective* forum where rational decisions about the future of the enterprise can be made. In order to achieve this outcome, a CEO must have a process.

Content Versus Process Consultants

A CEO who elects to seek outside assistance to help decide the future direction of the company is faced with having to choose between two very different types of consultants.

One is the "content" consultant. These are the traditional firms such as McKinsey, Bain, Boston Consulting Group, Monitor and many others. Their claim to fame is that they have "industry experts" who know their industry better than the client does. Their objective is to formulate a strategy *for* you since your people are not as knowledgeable as their "experts." In other words, they do it for you, or to you.

In our view, this form of consulting may be appropriate in regards to operational issues, but it is not appropriate to strategy and strategic direction. These firms are "content" consultants and they are selling content. Unfortunately, they sell the same content to all their clients in that industry. The best result is a "me-too" strategy that does not set you apart from your competitors and will never bring supremacy over them. You are, in our humble opinion, *outsourcing your thinking*.

A better service to a CEO and the management team, in our view, is to bring them a *process* and guide them through that process. However, it is *their* content going into the process and it is *their* content coming out. When the strategy has been constructed by the people who have the best content to offer and have a vital stake in the outcome, such a strategy gets implemented much more quickly and much more successfully than one that is imposed on them by an outside third party.

The CEO As Process Leader

"Follow me!" T.E. Lawrence shouted to his Arab troops as he led his army's charge into battle.

Although the term "leadership" is frequently used to describe successful CEOs, few executives in business today can be considered true leaders. The litmus test for any leader is whether he or she will be followed as Lawrence of Arabia was followed by an army of people who were not of his race or religion. For the followers to allow themselves to be led assumes their implicit belief in the leader's ability. Followers want to know where they are being led.

Many books have been written on leadership, but few have been able to describe it in comprehensive terms. Nor have they been able to describe the skills of leadership in any detail except to attribute it to a "trait of personality." John P. Kotter, in his 1988 book *The Leadership Factor,* explained that leadership can be defined, analyzed, and learned. He also pointed out that it is not taught in business schools. Unfortunately, he did not articulate in his book how leadership skills can be acquired.

Jack Welch, CEO of General Electric, views it this way in a *Business Week* interview:

> "A leader is someone who can develop a vision of what he or she wants their business, their unit, to do and be. Somebody who is able to articulate to the entire unit what the unit is and gain through a sharing of the discussion–listening and talking–an acceptance of that vision. And then can relentlessly drive implementation of that vision to a successful conclusion."

The flip side of this position was summed up by Roger Smith, former CEO of General Motors, in a *Fortune* interview. In explaining his failure to turn that company around more quickly, Smith cited the "inability to communicate his vision of General Motors earlier and more frequently" than he did.

Welch's definition of leadership is probably as close to the mark as any we could conjure up ourselves. However, hidden in this definition is the assumption that the CEO has mastered the skill of *strategic thinking*, the process used by a CEO to formulate, articulate, communicate, and successfully deploy a clear, concise, and explicit strategy for the organization.

A Fundamental Skill Of Leadership

Many CEOs are good strategic thinkers. The problem, however, is that they practice their skill by *osmosis* and are not conscious of its various elements and steps. As a result, they do not use the process systematically. They may also have great difficulty transmitting their ability to their subordinates. The reason is simple. Whatever cannot be described cannot be transferred.

Our experience at DPI suggests that most people who surround a CEO are not good strategic thinkers themselves. Again, the reason is simple. Managers are so engrossed in operational activity, so isolated in their functional silos, that they have not developed the ability to think strategically. A CEO, therefore, may wish to involve subordinates in a deliberate application of the Strategic Thinking Process strictly for its educational value for both the CEO and his or her subordinates.

The Role Of The CEO

There is only one person in any organization who can "drive" the Strategic Thinking Process and that is the chief executive of that organization. *Strategic thinking, then, must start with the CEO.* Strategic thinking is definitively a trickle-down process and not a bubble-up one. It is a very interactive process, but the CEO must be its owner. As such, the CEO must show commitment to the process by participating in all its phases and work sessions.

Because the process is highly interactive, it is not for the faint of heart. The process invites discussion, debate, and constructive provocation. Everyone, during its various phases, has the opportunity to express his or her views, have these challenged, and then challenge those of others. As a result, the process is ideal for CEOs who encourage frank, open discussion of issues and challenges.

A CEO has two options available to get a strategy implemented. The first approach is *compliance*. Here the CEO announces what the strategy is and how he or she expects it to be implemented. The CEO then assigns different tasks to different individuals. They, in turn, implement the strategy without questioning its rationale. In a world of increasing complexity, this approach has less and less appeal to more and more CEOs.

The second, and more effective, method is *commitment*. Here key executives actively participate in developing the rationale behind the strategy and assist the CEO in crafting the strategy itself. In order to ensure widespread commitment to the strategy, most CEOs include the top two levels of management in the process.

The Role Of The Process Facilitator

One role that the CEO should not attempt to play is that of *process facilitator*. One cannot have one foot in the process and one foot in the content. Attempting to guide the process while participating in the debate will give everyone the impression that the CEO is trying to manipulate the process to a predetermined conclusion. Therefore, it is wiser to have a third-party facilitator guide the process along.

A facilitator is not a *moderator*. A moderator is a person who directs traffic as well as he or she can during a meeting, but without relying on a specific process. By contrast, a facilitator is a trained professional who comes to each meeting with a *structured* process together with pre-designed instruments that keep the discussion moving forward in a constructive manner toward a specific set of conclusions. The facilitator also keeps the process honest, balanced, and objective.

As the CEO of a Fortune 10 company said to me during one of our work sessions, "You know, Mike, you're the only one in this room who tells me to sit down and I do. No one else in this room would dare say that to me."

The Process Is The Focal Point

However talented our people may be as facilitators, we never forget that it is the *process* which allows executives that we work with to formulate a supremacy strategy. An equally important aspect of strategy is not only its *formulation* but also its *deployment.* This is done through the development and resolution of *Critical Issues.*

Chapter 12

Strategy Deployment: Critical Issues

"It's easy to develop a strategy, it's the *implementation* that's difficult." This is a statement we have frequently heard over the years. Our own experience shows that the *formulation* of a strategy is as difficult as its implementation. However, many CEOs have difficulty getting people to implement their strategy for several reasons.

The Strategy Is Implicit And Not Explicit

In too many organizations, the strategy of the company is implicit and resides solely in the head of the chief executive. Most chief executives have a strategy. However, for reasons described in a previous chapter, they have great difficulty articulating it to the people around them.

One senior executive of a *Fortune 500* company once said to us, "The reason I have difficulty implementing my CEO's strategy is because I don't know what it is!"

Lesson #1: People cannot implement what they don't know.

Because many CEOs have difficulty verbalizing their strategy, most people are placed in the position of having to "guess" what the strategy is, and they may guess wrong as often as they guess right. Or else, they learn what the strategy is over time by the nature of the decisions they recommend which are either accepted or rejected. Gradually, a subordinate learns where the line of demarcation is between the things that are permitted by the strategy and those that are not. This is called *strategy*

136

by groping because the strategy becomes clear or explicit only over a long period of time, during which people may have spent too much time pursuing and implementing activities that did not fit while not paying enough attention to opportunities that represented a better strategic fit.

The Strategy Is Developed In Isolation

A second reason the strategy may not be implemented properly is that it was developed by the CEO in isolation. Many CEOs have a strategy, but their key people are not involved in the *process* and therefore have no ownership. In such a case, subordinates usually do not understand the rationale behind the strategy and will spend more time questioning it than implementing it. The CEO becomes more and more impatient as subordinates question his logic more and more often. The CEO, on the other hand, can't comprehend why his people are not executing what, to him, is a simple strategy.

> Lesson #2: People don't implement properly what they don't understand!

Some CEOs might involve one or two people in the formulation of the strategy. This is better than doing it alone but is still not good enough. The *entire* management team must be involved in order to achieve accurate understanding and proper execution.

As Dale Lang, chairman of *Working Woman* magazine, noted as a reason for using our strategic process: "I could have dictated to the staff what I wanted to do, but it's a whole lot better if they reach the conclusion themselves. In that way, they're working *their* plan and know how and why they chose it."

The Strategy Is Developed By An Outside Consultant

The worst of all strategic crimes and the "kiss of death" for any strategy–even a good one–is to have an outside consultant develop your strategy. No outside consultant has the right to set the direction of your organization or knows as much as your own people about the business and the environment it is facing. Most strategies developed by outside consultants end up in the wastepaper basket for two reasons:

1.   Everyone can quickly tear the conclusions apart because they are not based on an intimate knowledge of the company, the business, or the industry.

2.   There is no commitment to that strategy by senior management because it is not *their* strategy.

Experience has shown that almost any strategy will work, unless it is completely invalidated by negative environmental factors. Experience has also shown, however, that no strategy will work if a couple or a few members of senior management are not committed to that strategy. In effect, if total commitment is not present, those uncommitted to the strategy will, on a day-to-day basis, do everything in their power to prove it wrong.

> Lesson #3: People don't implement what they are not committed to.

In order to obtain commitment, key managers must be involved at each step of the process so that their views are heard and discussed. Participation, although sometimes time-consuming, builds commitment. Key managers buy into the strategy because they helped construct it. It is as much their strategy as the CEO's.

Many CEOs have used our process knowing the outcome in advance. They did so anyway, using it as a tool to tap the advice and knowledge of their people and to obtain commitment to the conclusion, so that implementation of the strategy can then proceed expeditiously.

Operational People Are Not Good Strategic Thinkers

Because most people spend their entire careers with an organization dealing exclusively with operational issues, they are not good strategic thinkers as noted earlier. With few exceptions, we have found that only the CEO or the general manager sees the "big picture" and views the business and its environment in strategic terms. There usually is only one strategist in any organization and that is the CEO. Most managers are so engrossed in operational activity that they have not developed the skill of thinking *strategically.* Therefore, they have difficulty coping with strategic issues, especially if these are sprung on them out-of-the-blue. "The problem," says Milton Lauenstein in an article in the *Journal of Business Strategy,* "is that many executives have only the fuzziest notion of the functions of strategy formulation."

Lesson #4: The CEO may encourage the participation of key subordinates in the strategic process for strictly educational value.

People will implement a strategy more effectively if they understand the difference between a strategic process and either long-range or operational planning, together with the difference between strategic and operational issues.

The Critical Issues Are Not Identified

One aspect of strategy is its formulation. Another is thinking through its implications. Most strategic planning systems we have seen used in organizations don't encourage people to think through the implications of their strategy. As a result, they end up reacting to these events as they are encountered and many people start losing faith in the strategy. "There were so many holes in the CEO's strategy, I gave up trying to implement it," is how a senior vice president of a major organization put it. Every strategy, especially if it represents a change of direction, has implications.

Lesson #5: People give up on a strategy whose implications have not been anticipated.

A good strategic process should help management identify and practically manage the strategy's implications on the company's products, markets, customers, organization structure, personnel, and culture.

Identification Of Critical Issues

Critical issues are the bridge between the current profile and the future strategic profile of an organization that management has deliberately decided to pursue. The direction of the organization has been decided, and

managing that direction begins. Managing that direction on an ongoing basis means management of the critical issues which stem from four key areas:

- Structure
- Systems/Processes
- Skills/Competencies
- Compensation.

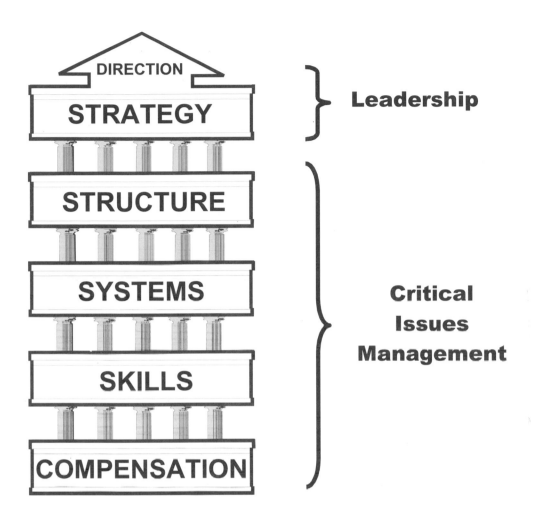

Critical Issues That Relate To Structure

One of our clients recently asked us a very good question: *Since most corporations are organized in a similar manner, does that mean that they have a similar strategy?*

After all, most companies have a Marketing function, a Sales function, a Production function, an Engineering function, an Accounting function, an IT function, a Human Resource function, etc. Most are also organized in a similar manner geographically with a domestic operational unit and an international unit separated by country, or groups of countries, into regions. They may further be organized by product by country which leads to some form of "matrix" organization. Therefore, *similar organization, similar strategy.*

Nothing could be further from the truth! Although organizational structures look as if they stem from the same business model, there are some important nuances that make the various functions behave in very different modes. A correlating example is people. Although all men wear suits and all women wear dresses, no two women or two men behave in the same way.

The same is true in business. Although all companies "wear" the same clothes–organization–no two organizations behave in the same manner in the marketplace. In fact, if you were to look more carefully, you would detect that, although companies use the same words or titles, they are in fact organized in a very *different* manner.

The underlying element that determines an organization's structure is the concept of Driving Force which is at the root of every business strategy.

Take, for example, 3M, Johnson & Johnson and Caterpillar, the examples used earlier. 3M is organized around "applications" it uncovers for its knowledge of polymer chemistry-its *Driving Force.* As a result, it has a Post-it Division, a Masking Tape Division, a Video Tape division, a Film Division... which are all different applications of its root polymer chemistry. Each division has its own sales, marketing, and manufacturing functions since these tend to require *different skills* from one application to another using *different* methods to get to market. Some divisions sell direct, some use agents and distributors. Some make end-use products, some make components for other companies' products.

TECHNOLOGY–DRIVEN ORGANIZATION

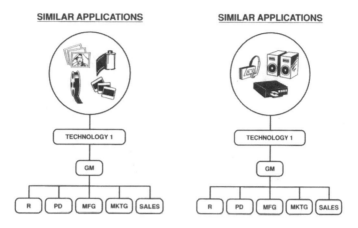

Caterpillar, on the other hand, uses the same titles and words but is organized in a very different manner. Since it pursues a *product-driven* strategy–earthmoving machines–the company is organized around different product categories. They have a Large Machine Division, a Mid-size Machine Division, a Small Machine Division and recently added a Compact Machine Division. The manufacturing is decentralized whereby different functions are centralized and broken down geographically with a General Manager for each geographic market. This is done to accommodate Caterpillar's unique network of Independent Dealers which is their chosen way to market.

PRODUCT–DRIVEN ORGANIZATION

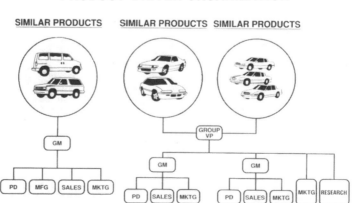

Johnson & Johnson is not organized like either of the above. Its strategy is "satisfying the health needs of doctors, nurses, patients and mothers" – *a user class driven* strategy. As such, it is organized around where these four individuals are accessed. As a result, it has two divisions – a Hospital Division since this is where doctors, nurses and patients are found, and it has a Consumer Division which is where the mother is found. Manufacturing is thus centralized while each division has its own Sales & Marketing organizations. All the products aimed at doctors, nurses and patients go through the Hospital Division and all the products aimed at mothers go through the Consumer Division.

USER CLASS–DRIVEN ORGANIZATION

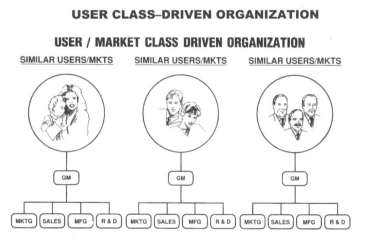

There was a fad in the 1970s and 1980s to reorganize and restructure companies. After the reorganization, the difficult question to answer became: "Now that we are reorganized, where are we going?"

In our view, structure follows strategy. The organization structure of the business must support the direction of that business. We have further learned that each Driving Force requires a slightly different organization structure.

Critical Issues That Relate To Processes/Systems

The next discussion that leads to critical issues is one that revolves around the subject of "systems." Many companies today have purchased sophisticated and costly electronic information systems only to find out some time later that the systems are not supportive of the company's business strategy. Again, our view is that all information systems must be aligned with the direction of the organization and that there are usually issues that surface in the area of systems or processes.

Critical Issues That Relate To Skills/Competencies

When an organization changes its direction, this change will usually require the acquisition of a new set of skills. These can be developed, but frequently they do not reside in-house and must be acquired, thus giving rise to another set of critical issues.

Critical Issues That Relate To Compensation

In spite of all the titles or power you might think you have over people, my experience has convinced me that people do not do what you want them to do; people do what they are *paid* to do. If your strategy says that you want your people to behave in a certain manner, but your compensation system rewards them to do something different, I can bet almost anything that at the end of the year they will have done what they were *paid* to do and not what you *wanted* them to do.

As a result, another area of discussion that raises critical issues is the subject of compensation, to ensure that the compensation of key individuals is geared to supporting the strategy and direction of the business.

Around these four areas–structure, systems, skills, and compensation–a number of critical issues are identified and assigned to specific individuals for resolution. The results expected are articulated, the macro action steps are listed, other people that need to be involved are assigned to each team, and completion and review dates are established. These critical issues then become "the plan" for the organization, and it is the ongoing management and resolution of these issues that makes the CEO's vision a reality over time. It is how the strategy is deployed successfully.

Closing The Loop

At this point, you might be wondering how all the concepts presented tie together into a cohesive whole.

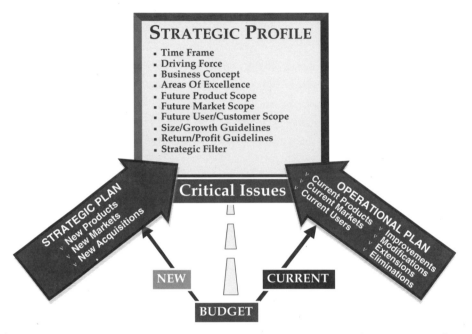

The rectangle at the top of the graphic represents the output of our *Strategic Thinking Process*. The strategic profile is a description of what an organization wants to look like at some point in the future. The inside of the rectangle contains the content of this picture. The critical issues are the bridge that needs to be crossed in order to go from what the company looks like today to what it wants to look like tomorrow. Now comes planning time.

The Operational Plan

At this point in the process, one needs to examine the organization's current activities and decide which products, customers, and markets need to be improved or modified. Moreover, one must identify those that need to be eliminated because they no longer fit the vision of what the company is trying to become.

One of the most difficult decisions we find management having to make is not what to do but rather what *not to do anymore*. This is because there is always someone telling management to "hang in" a little longer–that the corner is about to come but, in fact, it never does. During the operational planning stage, these decisions become easier to make, because all participants have agreed that those activities no longer fit their aspiration of the type of company they are trying to build.

The Strategic Plan

In our view, a strategic plan is one that will alter the "look" of an organization in the future. The key elements that will alter the "look" of a company in the future are the new products, new customers, and new markets that the company wants to add to that look. A plan now needs to be constructed to make these happen.

Our experience shows that if you want to give birth to brand new activities (products, markets and acquisitions), it is wise to have people other than those who are running your current businesses "midwife" these projects to birth. The rationale is simple: Those running your current businesses have a locomotive on their hands, and keeping that engine on track will require all their time and energy. As such, it is wise to have new activities managed outside the normal structure of the current business.

The Strategic Profile Is The Target For All Decisions

As illustrated, the strategic profile becomes the target for all the decisions that are made in the organization. Plans and decisions that fit inside the frame of this profile are pursued, and those that do not fit are not.

Chapter 13

Three
Strategic Processes
That Promote Supremacy

As our name, Decision Processes International (DPI for short), implies, everything we do revolves around *decisions*. Our mission is to uncover the *thinking processes* that senior executives employ to arrive at conclusions while conducting their business. To date, we have uncovered three different thinking processes that we believe are *critical* to the success of the business over time. We put these three processes under an umbrella we call *Critical Thinking*.

Strategic Thinking

The first and foremost responsibility of any CEO is to formulate a strategy for the organization in order to give its employees a sense of direction and harness their energy towards the goal of *supremacy* over its competitors. The process that assists a CEO in this endeavor is one that is proprietary to DPI which we call *Strategic Thinking*.

This process starts with the construction of a "snapshot" of the company in its present form. This consists of identifying the characteristics that are common to all the company's products, all the company's customers, all the company's market segments and all the company's geographic markets. By identifying the characteristics that are *common* across these four elements of a company's profile, we can then uncover the company's *current* Driving Force, its *current* Business Concept and its *current* Areas of Excellence. Having agreement about the company's *current* Profile is the starting point of *strategy formulation*.

The next step in this process is to conduct a scan of the external environment and determine what the Future Business Arena that we will find ourselves in, will look like. Once we are reasonably comfortable with that "picture" of the future, we can more specifically identify the *strategic variables* that will play for or against us in that arena. This will help us circumscribe the "sandbox" over which we want to establish supremacy.

Now for the fun part. Which "stealth" competitor could step into that sandbox and attempt to establish supremacy for itself and create havoc for us? One team is given this assignment and they develop a specific strategy and business model that such a "stealth" entrant would deploy against us.

The next step is then for us to identify which components of our business could be the Driving Force of our future strategy. Companies can usually identify 2 or 3 areas which could be the engine of their future strategy. We then take each of these "possible" Driving Forces and we develop "profiles" of what we would emphasize more or emphasize less under each one. The development of these scenarios then allows the CEO and the management team to choose the Driving Force that will best all current competitors, as well as any new "stealth" entrant into our sandbox.

The final step in this first work session is then to surface the Critical Issues that the management team will need to address and resolve over time in order to attain, maintain, or enhance our supremacy in our chosen sandbox.

Strategic Product Innovation

The strategy of a company is usually deployed through a continuous stream of new products that come from an overflowing hopper. Strategic supremacy is highly dependent on the organization's ability to create and bring to market new products more often and more quickly than its competitors. We view new product creation as the *fuel of corporate longevity*. DPI has developed a unique process in this area as well which is called *Strategic Product Innovation*. This process is used by the organization to create and commercialize new-to-the-market products (not seen before) that will generate new revenue streams and allow the company to grow faster than its competitors.

Our research in this area of corporate endeavor has uncovered ten sources from which can emerge new-to-the-market product concepts. These consist of:

- Unexpected successes
- Unexpected failures
- Unexpected external events
- Process weaknesses
- Industry/structural changes
- High growth stimulators
- Converging technologies
- Demographic shifts
- Perception shifts
- New knowledge

By exploring each of these ten areas, and their derivatives, management can generate dozens, if not hundreds, of new-to-the-market products. We have one client that generated over 1200 new product concepts by involving 200 of their best minds in this process.

The second step consists of ranking all these new product concepts in terms of their potential for the company. This is done by anticipating the relationship between:

- cost
- benefit
- strategic fit
- ease/difficulty of commercialization
- risk/reward ratio

Judging all concepts on these criteria allows management to rank them in order of attractiveness to the organization. Some of the new concepts with lesser potential are abandoned after this step. The remainder are then taken through the next step which consists of attempting to anticipate the *critical factors* that would cause each new product to *succeed* or *fail* in the marketplace.

The final step is to construct a commercialization plan that incorporates actions that will *prevent failure* and *ensure success.*

e-Strategy Process

The third critical thinking process required in today's world, we call e-*Strategy* and, again, it is unique and proprietary to DPI. This process allows management to construct a coherent "blueprint" consisting of specific applications leveraging the Internet's 12 e-nablers (capabilities). This process is another tool available to management to deploy its *business* strategy. Each application is chosen on the basis of its contribution towards the goal of achieving supremacy over the company's competitors.

This process also considers how the company's *competitors* will use the Internet and which e-nablers *they* would employ and the type of application they would develop. These applications then become ours and are incorporated into our blueprint.

This process has its own version of the "stealth" competitor that we call the *killer.com* newcomer. One team is given the mandate to develop a killer.com scenario and, again, their best applications are built into our blueprint. This blunts the killer.com entrant and enhances our supremacy in our chosen sandbox.

An Overall Project

Almost 98% of our clients stay clients forever. Many use all of our Critical Thinking processes "packaged" together into one project. Or they may introduce them to the organization one at a time. When a client decides to take senior executives from different levels through all of our processes, the logistics of how such a project might unfold would look like this:

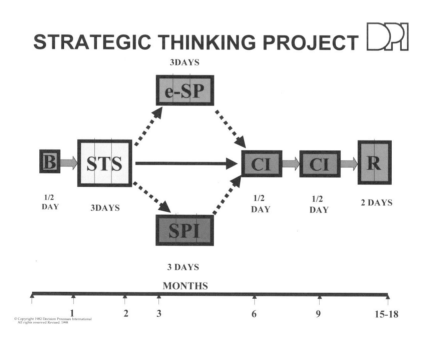

As shown on the time scale, a project including the three processes will take 15 to 18 months. This does not mean that we invade your domain and stay on site with an army of junior consultants for that period of time. Rather, there are five phases to such a project and they can be described in the following manner:

Phase 1 – Briefing

A project usually starts with the CEO and the key members of the management team going through the Strategic Thinking Process. This is the process which results in the formulation of a *supremacy strategy*.

Phase 1 is a 3-hour briefing session which has two activities:

- Give the management team an overview of the concepts and process of Strategic Thinking so that they are "at ease" with these.
- Each member is then given a Strategic Analysis Input Survey and asked to answer its 14 categories of questions. This requires 3 to 4 hours of work and is spread over two weeks. We ask that they answer the survey without consulting each other. Our objective is to extract each person's best thinking on all key elements of the organization's current status as well as each person's perception of the future environment which will confront the organization. The answers are then sent to us for collating and editing.

Phase 2 – The Strategic Thinking Supremacy Work Session

This 3-day work session is the focal point of a project. It is in this session that all key decisions are made about the future direction of the enterprise.

During the 3 days, the group is taken through the following process:

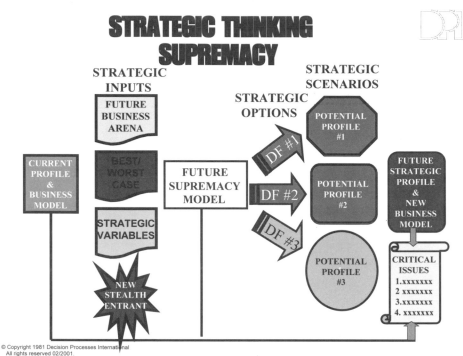

The outputs of this session are:

- An understanding of the company's current strategy and business model

- A description of the Future Business Arena that the company will find itself in

- A description of the Best Case and Worst Case Circumstances that the company might encounter in that Business Arena

- The identification of the "significant few" variables that will play for or against the organization in that Business Arena

- The identification of likely "stealth disruptors"

- Identification and assignment of Critical Issues which become the "work plan" for management. The resolution of these Issues is what will move the organization from where it is today to where it wants to be tomorrow.

Project Crossroads

After the completion of Phase 2, a project can take several paths.

1. One could skip Phases 3A and 3B and continue with Phases 4 and 5 applied only to the Strategic Thinking module, or
2. The CEO could decide that the company's hopper of new product opportunities is not sufficient and then proceed with the Strategic Product Innovation module, or
3. The CEO is concerned about the advent of the Internet and its possible impact on the business and there is no coherent blueprint in place and, therefore, wishes to proceed with the e-Strategy module, or
4. The CEO sees a need for both modules.

Phase 3A – Strategic Product Innovation Work Session

The objective of this process is to create and develop commercialization plans for as many new-to-the-market products as can be generated by the best "product creators" the company has.

The Process of New Product Innovation & Introduction

©Copyright 1987 Decision Processes International
All rights reserved. Revised 1995, 1999

The group will be taken through the following process:

Search

In this step we will examine the types of changes that bring opportunities to an organization. We will identify a number of such changes that are affecting your organization and attempt to convert these into concepts for:

- New-to-the-market products
- New customers
- New markets

Assessment

The second step will then attempt to rank these opportunities to determine their degree of attractiveness for the business. These will be judged on the basis of:
- Cost
- Benefit
- Strategic fit
- Difficulty of implementation

Development

In this third step, we will take the opportunities that will have emerged as being the most attractive and develop them further considering the following elements:

- The best-case outcomes
- The worst-case outcomes
- The risk/reward ratio

These steps will allow us to then focus our efforts on "la crème de la crème" of the total inventory of opportunities.

Pursuit

The fourth and final step will then be to construct a successful commercialization plan for the very best opportunities by:

- Identifying the critical factors that will cause the best and worst outcomes to materialize.
- Identifying preventive actions that will avoid the worst-case outcomes.
- Identifying promotive actions that will encourage the best-case outcomes to materialize.
- Constructing an implementation plan that incorporates both preventive and promotive actions.

Phase 3B – e-Strategy Work Session

The objective of this work session is to create a "blueprint" of Internet-based applications that will contribute to enhancing the company's supremacy over its competitors.

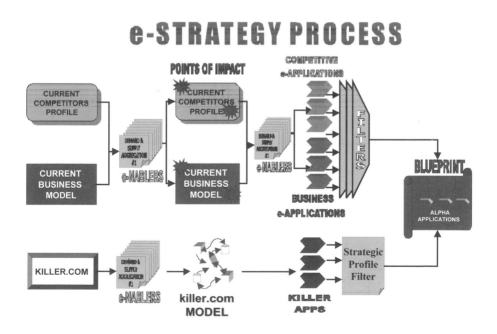

The intent of this process is to make your people the "architects" who determine "what" you want done and the solution provider the "engineer" who determines "how" to do it. In this manner you increase substantially the probability of developing a distinctive e-strategy that will provide you with an additional advantage over your competitors and enhance your supremacy.

This work session will produce the following outputs:

- An overall, coherent corporate "blueprint" describing *where* and *how* the company should use the Internet.
- Identification of ways whereby competitors might use the Internet to their advantage.
- Identification of ways to use the Internet to "change the game" and create your own rules.
- A set of concrete internet, intranet and extranet "specs" that can be used to guide the work of the hardware and software provider you choose to implement the solutions you will have designed.

Phase 4 – Critical Issues Meeting

One CEO client recently said to this author:
"You DPI guys are no more than *strategic enforcers*. Because we scheduled a meeting with you, we show up. Otherwise, we'd find something else to do. And when we show up, we know what questions you are going to ask. So we work our butts off because no one wants to go to that meeting and report 'no progress.' " I thought this was a very good way of describing our involvement in the *deployment* of the strategy as well as in its *formulation*.

Phase 4 consists of two quarterly, _ day meetings with the CEO and the management team to review progress on the Critical Issues. At these meetings, the "owner" of each issue is expected to give a report of progress. These meetings give the CEO an opportunity to:

- assess the progress, or non-progress, on each issue
- determine whether the issue is "on-track" or "off-track"

- judge whether the work on each issue is proceeding at the proper pace
- remove any obstacles that the owners and their teams are running into
- make any midcourse corrections

Phase 5 – Review/Revisit Session

Some 10 to 12 months after Phase 2, most clients want to have a review, or revisit, of their previous conclusions. Because these conclusions were based on a certain number of assumptions as to what might or might not occur in the environment, most CEOs want to revisit these assumptions to see which proved to be right and which ones wrong. This reassessment allows the client to fine-tune the strategy and occasionally pick up a Critical Issue or two that were missed the first time through the process.

Summary

The Critical Issues that come out of Phase 2, the New Product Plans that come out of Phase 3A, and the Internet Applications that come out of Phase 3B are all merged into one master list of Strategic Issues that become the working agenda for each Management Committee meeting. These issues are the bridge which the organization needs to cross to achieve *strategic supremacy*. DPI stays involved in the process until the client is well on the way to getting across that bridge.

Conclusion

"Thinking," said Henry Ford, "is a difficult activity. That is why so many people don't practice that habit."

We could not have said it better. Our challenge at DPI is to make common sense, common practice. Give us a call. We can help you achieve strategic supremacy in your sandbox by outthinking your competitors.

Chapter 14

CEOs Speak Their Minds On The Value Of Strategic Thinking

Our company, Decision Processes International, publishes a magazine entitled *The Strategist* which is sent to 40,000 CEOs six times per year.

First published in 1990, each issue has carried an interview with one of our client CEOs which means that over 70 CEOs have appeared on its cover.

This book contains four full interviews with CEOs who have used the concepts and process described therein. In this section, however, you will find excerpts from 20 other CEOs who have been featured in previous issues of *The Strategist*. Although our work with these CEOs occurred during different periods of time, their comments about our process and its results are remarkably similar. The concepts have also proven to be culture free and transcend both industries and geography.

We have included the first three "mini-interviews" because they provide a variety of insights which will offer excellent guidance to CEOs looking to improve their chances of achieving strategic supremacy.

Following the API, Bekaert, and OM Group stories, we have also extracted the most salient thoughts of a wide range of strategic thinkers. We hope you find their ideas and insights to be helpful to you in running your business.

American Precision Industries   **API Motion**
Kurt Wiedenhaupt
Former CEO

Building a Vision for the Future

An Expert's View Of The Strategic Thinking Process

As the first client of Decision Process International back in the 1980's, Kurt Wiedenhaupt has a unique perspective on the Strategic Thinking Process. An acquaintance of Mike Robert at the time, he learned of the process when Mike visited his home in the United Kingdom.

Wiedenhaupt was intrigued by the concepts that Mike showed him and he decided to try out the DPI Process on the management team of AEG, the company he was with at the time. It was so successful in creating a cohesive strategy that he used the process several more times to help management teams sort out strategies in subsequent assignments. He had identified something new in the DPI process that was a refreshing change from other methods of strategy creation he had encountered.

"I have been exposed to McKinsey, Boston Consulting Group, and to Bain & Co. They are all very capable and I'm sure they have a good product that's extremely impressive," he says "and I'm sure intellectually they're also very sound. The only problem is their product is not of the people, by the people, through the people, for the people. It's not owned by the people who later have to live with it. When the strategy is developed by an outside third party, it is an alien product no matter how well it relates to the company. That's why it fails, even if they come up with a better product than the process we are using. But when it comes to executing it, they are miles behind DPI. It's simply ownership. We as human beings do what we *believe* in, and we do that with *enthusiasm*. If somebody else tells us something to do, we might do it, but don't expect any enthusiasm.

"But anyone who is considering using the process, should not see it as a one time exercise, it has to become part of the company, part of the everyday life, language like Critical Issues, Driving Force, Areas of

Excellence, Strategic Thinking, becomes part of our daily verbiage. This is part of our language, part of our culture, we live with it, and it gets stronger and stronger."

Strategy And The New CEO

Having been called upon several times in his career to take the reins of businesses he did not know as an insider, Wiedenhaupt has come to recognize that Strategic Thinking can be an especially valuable tool to the CEO coming into a new situation–either as incoming Chief Executive or in the integration of a new acquisition.

"This process, I have found through my own experience," he says, "can be beautifully used by *any* new CEO coming into a company or business he is not fully familiar with. You have the opportunity in a very short period of time to immerse yourself into this new business. You get a deep understanding of the issues. You get a very good feeling for the players in your organization who are participating in this process. And I have to say it took at least half a year out of the learning process in my last assignment. I feel much more secure in the path I'm walking because my own people have described that path and they are walking with me."

N. V. Bekaert, S.A.   ⬚ **BEKAERT**
Rafaël Decaluwé
CEO

Rewiring a Global Strategy

"After interviewing and debating with a number of people, not the least of which were the people on the board–who look at my rating sheet and my pay every year–I came to the conclusion that my primary task is shaping the vision of the company, communicating it and getting it implemented. Now those are three things that are easily said, but not so easily done," he says.

His perception at the time was that the company was strong operationally, yet needed a vision of the future to drive and grow its performance in the future. He looked at "solution-driven" consultants whom, he believed, would run the risk of not understanding the business, jumping to conclusions and, most importantly, achieving low credibility with management. He settled on a different approach–in the form of the DPI Strategic Thinking Process. "What I wanted was a methodology that involved the thinking of our own people. I would hope that the people who were working in this business for 20 and more years would have a better view and understanding of what this business is capable of doing and where it should go, than an outside consultant who comes for three to six months, reviews and interviews your people, and then comes up with a so-called magic solution of what you should do for the next 'x' years.

"I was a firm believer after my previous experiences that a team comes up with better answers than an individual, and, therefore, if you can involve a team in that sort of thinking about strategy, your commitment of the group, having contributed to it, will be far larger and will make the implementation easier. I would certainly stand by that. So it starts from the philosophy of a CEO. In my own view you must feel that, yes, you are CEO, but you also realize that as one individual, given the size of the company, you're in no way physically capable of managing and directing strategy and all the operational issues yourself. So I recognize my own limitations from a physical and intellectual point of view as my starting point on building an organization with a team. In that context, I have found the Strategic Thinking approach extremely helpful.

"If you ask me now what were the advantages of the Strategic Thinking Process, I was really looking for something that would force our people to think and come up with some answers," says Decaluwé. "It did bring us much closer and the team definitely functioned much better. It gave us consensus. It led us to focus on a few critical issues. We started out with a long list and got it down to five. It led the whole group to take on ownership. And on top of that it is applicable to any level. Not only can you do it for the group, you can do it for business units.

"I call it a 'do-it-yourself kit' for managers in terms of coming to think about where you are with your business and taking hold of it."

OM Group
Jim Mooney
CEO

The Importance of Strategic Focus

"It's probably the greatest war game in the world," says Jim Mooney, president and CEO of the OM Group. "You create a vision, develop a stronger army, bring on new weapons and generate new growth. You don't let any of your people get hurt and it's all non-violent. How much more fun can you have?"

Vision Attracts Investment

"We've been well received by the markets for two reasons," Mooney continues. "The first is our performance which has been very good. The second is that we've been able to communicate our business in a way that the market can understand. Without the Strategic Thinking Process helping us, that story would not have been as clear.

"For the first time we had a uniform identity for the company. Because of this the Finnish owners were more comfortable that we were capable of bringing it to the marketplace. And it made the investment bankers more comfortable because they really understood our key drivers for growth and earnings.

"The easiest way to describe our business is with the concepts developed through the Strategic Thinking Process," says Mooney. "The best thing about it is you don't have to give away your secrets, but you do let them know how you think. They know that they're buying a metal-based specialty chemical company with growth opportunities. It's real simple, that's what we are. We're nothing more than that. We're not going to look at anything else. They know that we have a global presence. They know that we have ongoing new product development, that we have an advanced and proprietary production capability. They know that we have long-term reliable supply relationships which feed that production capability. They know they're buying into a company with experienced management that understands the external environment as well as the internal environment. They understand how we focus on niche markets and what areas we want to go into, what areas we don't want to go into, based on our strategic focus and discipline. They know where we want to expand our existing product range. They know where targets are for new product development, and that strategic acquisitions have to fit the criteria that we just developed in front of them.

"The investors can see we have absolute discipline in our focus, and that there is no variation off of that. We're getting ready to do a public issue," Mooney explains. "And if I didn't have the concepts developed through Strategic Thinking, I don't know how I would explain this thing. The first thing they always tell us about our business is it's too complicated, you go to 30 markets and you have 250 products. You have global capabilities. You're buying material out of Congo and Zambia, which are politically unstable. And they can give you a million reasons why they can't buy our stock. But once we go through the operational strategy that we use to run our business, show them our vision strategy without giving away the secrets, address some critical issues, that simplifies the business real quick. Growth through metal-based specialty chemicals, period, nothing more than that. Niche markets, new product development, global expansion, acquisitions, it's pretty clear what we're going to do. They don't want a public relations firm telling them what OMG is doing, they want to hear it direct."

In Jim Mooney's view, too many companies suffer from a *lack* of vision or a distinctive strategy. This hurts their chances of growing *and* convincing potential investors and customers that they will grow. Relying on "spin doctors" to position the company's story is no substitute, he feels.

"I'll go to presentations and someone will be talking about how important their investor relations or public relations department is. And I'm sitting there thinking, 'My God, if you've got to talk about that, you've forgotten what you're in business for. You don't really have a vision. You're trying to create a vision where there isn't one.' Investors will support you with a clear vision. They won't support you if all you've got is a public relations manager. People see right through that. I can't tell you how many companies I see that have good operations people, but they have no vision as to where the company's going, what's driving it. They'll actually say,

'Well, you know, we had a bad quarter last one, we may have a bad quarter this one, but we're doing everything we can, we're going to fix it.' I'm sitting there thinking, 'Holy cow, how can you even go to work like that?' "

After the IPO: Acquiring To The Driving Force

Since the beginning, OMG has pursued a plan to grow in three areas: acquisitions, new products, and geographic reach. Guided by strategic filters, clearly agreed upon by the entire management team, OM Group appears to be succeeding in making the plan work. This built-in compass helps them target only opportunities that leverage their production capability.

"When our people develop products or look at markets or identify acquisitions, they know exactly where we're headed, they know what we're looking for," says Mooney. "Now when they see an acquisition and they bring it to my attention whether this fits in, whether it's metal-based specialty chemicals, whether it's something we can leverage with our production. We don't want to get into a me-too application. We look for new product potential, whether it offers new niches, whether it fortifies the current weaknesses we have or builds on strengths.

"The first item on my agenda in running the business is to look at their operational objectives and understand them," he says. "The second order of business is to put them through the Strategic Thinking Process. The pure reason why we do this is so that everybody understands where the company is headed. It builds trust, it builds confidence, it builds opportunities, it addresses weaknesses in a very positive way. This process has the unique capability of enabling you to look at your own plan and have bullets going through you and you don't feel bad about it."

Grasping The Big Picture

"At first everybody thinks that they understand strategy," Mooney says. "Yet they confuse operations and the vision, and what the larger Critical Issues are that have to be addressed, and what you have to do in your strategic profile to get where you want to be. After that's all laid out and there are disagreements on it and it's hashed out, there seems to be a point of consensus. At that point of consensus the Critical Issues that need to be accomplished can be addressed very easily. In a matter of days you can get a whole management group there. At the end of the Strategic Thinking session they understand what your Driving Force is, they understand what Areas of Excellence you have."

CATERPILLAR®

Caterpillar, Inc.
George Schaeffer & Don Fites, Former CEOs
Glen Barton, CEO

George Schaeffer

"We were foundering despite help from the top consultants available. We had too much good advice."

Don Fites

"This was the late 80's. We'd experienced a decade without really any shareholder value being created…survival was a word we talked about around here."

"I think the DPI process was exactly the right approach to take because ours is a company where most of the people spend their lifetime. We're very attached to the business and the equipment. We know the market and the customers. We know the business very well, and it's not a business that is easy to grasp. I mean, there aren't a whole lot of companies, there aren't really any companies in the world like Caterpillar. We don't have any models to follow. Forcing us to do that assessment process was exactly the right thing because only we, in the end, could have made that assessment, arrived at the conclusions and took the path that we eventually did."

"I think the whole idea of someone from the outside telling people who have spent their whole life in a company that something will or won't work is not really a good idea. They don't have the insight into what makes the company tick. The thing this process does very well, and I've seen it done over and over, it forces you to come up with the good news and the bad news. And *you* find the answers to these issues yourselves."

"*This is not a process for wimps*. It is not a process where somebody is going to tell you how to save or maybe even improve your organization. But it is a process that if you go into it recognizing that you've got to change, that you've got to do better–if you want to maintain your leadership *or even survive*–this process, better than any I've seen, will get the job done."

"As far as the shareholders are concerned, it's the creation of shareholder value which has been rather spectacular."

"I think it is one of the truly remarkable success stories of the 1990's. The track record is there in terms of financial results, market shares... percentage of sales...the whole nine yards."

Glen Barton

"We went through a number of consultants who worked with us. Among several others we had the top strategy consultant at the time, Michael Porter, and Noel Tichy, who was a facilitator who had worked with General Electric on their break-out process…Rather than spending two or three years getting the background that a traditional strategy consultant like Porter might have wanted we felt the DPI Process was a much more straightforward approach that we would be comfortable with and get faster results, which at the time was important."

"Some of these consulting projects never seem to end. They just keep rolling and rolling and getting bigger and bigger, and longer and longer, and more involved… In the last ten years we have used DPI's Strategic Thinking Process many times and when we undertake it we know there's an end. And when we get to that end, there are decisions we're going to make and directions we're going to take and move on from that."

"The Process drove us through considerations of what kind of company we wanted to be–product-driven, market-driven or technology or manufacturing-driven. We finally arrived, through the process, at what we thought we were–and still are–a product-driven company."

"I think the reorganization is the most significant thing that has happened as a direct result of the DPI Process, and I think we had a total turnaround in our company in recent years as a result of it."

3M Corporation, Protective Materials Division
Mike Harnetty
3M Worldwide
Division Vice President

"The DPI process was very, very effective for us. This was partly because we were not an organization who wanted some consulting expert to come in and tell us how to do our business. We were extremely successful at it. We knew it better than anybody. What we needed was a facilitator, or a referee to get the argument started, get the juices flowing, to let people say what they thought, and then, put a process on the table that allows them to think all of that through and deal with it. Then you aren't going home with everybody firmly entrenched in *their* thinking, with nobody's mind changed at all."

"In that whole discussion, probably the single biggest discovery was this Driving Force concept. What is your Driving Force? *What is the one thing*? Your Driving Force is the one thing you do better than anyone else, or the one thing that makes you unique. And identifying that Driving Force led us to the conclusion that that's what we needed to protect."

"One conclusion the DPI process brought us to was that we needed to begin prioritizing our businesses, and evaluating the opportunities they presented in the light of our Driving Force and our competitive threats. This led us, very early on, to decide to get out of some businesses. There were two or three businesses that we were in for reasons that nobody could remember other than, 'We're in them so we've got to participate in them.' And it laid the groundwork for some decisions soon after that. We said, 'Here's four or five businesses or product lines that we should not be in,' and the reason was that they were not connected to our Driving Force."

"You'd better understand what your strength is, focus on what you're good at. If you're not good at anything, then you've got to question why you're in this business. But if you're fortunate enough to find something that you're unique at, have a better chance of winning than anyone else, then that's what you build on. That becomes the cornerstone of the business. And all of your strategy should flow out of exploiting that, or protecting it. It gets to be pretty simple in a hurry actually."

Material Sciences Corporation   MSC Material Sciences Corporation
G. Robert Evans
Chairman & CEO

"The best leaders I have known really care about the development of people, really care about people's decision processes."

"When we begin to talk about a comprehensive long-term approach to strategic planning, it was apparent that we didn't have one. We had done good planning, but a lot of it was just very good operating extrapolations. We were looking for someone to come in and challenge our prior methods, analysis and conclusions with respect to the future."

"DPI's Strategic Thinking Process doesn't get bogged down in tactical issues like market situation analysis exercises. The Process puts the emphasis on thinking versus planning. ...Some consultants actually develop a plan, deliver it to you and tell you it's the plan you ought to execute. DPI doesn't do that. They provided a thinking process that enabled us to create the strategy ourselves."

"In one operation we had essentially ignored our Driving Force–our unique production capability. We have concentrated capital and human resources on developing that production capability in that unit and now it's doing marvelously."

"I think every organization, no matter what size, could really benefit from going through the exercises of identifying the Driving Force, the Areas of Excellence, Business Concept and Critical Issues."

NorAm Energy
Milt Honea
Chairman, President & CEO

"We needed to develop and, perhaps equally important, to effectively communicate a clear vision of what we wanted NorAm to look like ten years or so into the future, and what we as a company needed to do in terms of investment priorities and development of new competencies to achieve that vision."

"We liked the DPI approach because it draws on the knowledge and experience of our people rather than attempting, as some consulting firms tend to, to convince us of their view of the future and how they would position the company. By using our own people and our ideas we have been able to achieve total buy-in to those responsible for implementing our strategy—our own team."

"We owe a debt of gratitude to DPI. DPI had the right process at the right time for NorAm. NorAm is not the same company that it was when we began the DPI Process."

Groupe Cantrex, Inc.
Claude Lalonde
President

"We were a bit skeptical that we could come to a consensus with thirty managers participating. It's difficult enough to get consensus with five or six people sitting around a table…but we did come to a consensus and were very pleased with the result."

"We decided to change the rules of play in our market…now we're feeling the impact. It's an amazing change of direction."

Uniboard
Serge Bragdon
CEO

"My belief is that the best strategy is the one that people believe in, because then they are driven to achieve it. You can have the best strategy on paper, but if nobody is driven to achieve it, you don't succeed. I believe that to be successful the people must be part of the process."

"Some consultants come in and pick everyone's brains and put on paper what they *think* everyone *thinks*. But you try to push that down to people and it's not *their* strategy. It's what some one *else* thinks is their strategy. DPI's way works much better."

Pulte Corporation   **PULTE**
Robert Burgess
CEO

"We brought our corporate and field management teams together to candidly assess our strengths and areas of competitive advantage. We wanted the best input and complete buy-in from our entire senior management team."

"While we started out with a multitude of approaches and ideas, we ended up very strongly in agreement."

"The three-day Strategic Thinking Process is only the tip of the iceberg. The real benefit of going through this process is what happens in the weeks and months that follow. It has caused us to raise our level of strategic thinking both in the field and at the corporate office."

"The emphasis is as much on what you shouldn't spend your time on as on what you should be doing. There's no doubt we're much more focused on long-term growth in shareholder value."

Behlen Manufacturing Company
Tony Raimondo
CEO

"The Strategic Thinking Process walks everybody through a logical process that helps them sort out the company's strengths and weaknesses, and reach a unified conclusion about the Driving Force which makes us unique as a business. It's surprising. Most of our people were betting that we would not come to a unified conclusion."

"As a group, we were fragmented before going through this process. We had a small group that thought we were technology-driven, and a much larger group that thought we were production capacity-driven. We also had a group that thought we were a distribution company. Within the business units, we depend on autonomous thinking, and most of us believed that there was no common thread or Driving Force joining the units together. I was hoping that Strategic Thinking would bring out a common thread, and it did that marvelously well."

"I see the management team being able to sort through possible acquisitions much more easily–what's a good fit, what may be a fit and what potential acquisitions should be thrown away. It has greatly reduced the time it takes to say, 'Let's take a second look, or let's pass.' And that's because it's now easier to evaluate whether an acquisition will support or contribute to our Driving Force–our unique production capability."

"In my corporate background at General Motors, Moog (an aerospace company) and Sperry Corporation, we were involved in all kinds of traditional strategic planning methods, like the Boston Consulting Group and PIMS, etc. I think that kind of planning, coming from a corporate strategic planning group as such, is history. DPI's approach is a thinking process that allows you to continually modify and change. It doesn't tell you you're a cow to be milked or a star that has to do this or that. It puts a thinking process into the hands of real-world operations people. And that's the way to get strategic advantage from my point of view."

Union Pacific Resources
Jack Messman
Former CEO

"Our company sells a commodity product. We had doubts about the applicability of the DPI Process to a company which did not have an industrial or consumer product. Commodity products are not managed in the same way...however, we found the DPI Process did apply to our company, despite a commodity orientation. Using DPI's Process we developed a very successful strategy."

"It basically showed us that if you follow the DPI Process, the answers to your strategic questions exist in the minds of your own management team. The process helps you get it articulated and decided. It's a systematic approach which, when properly facilitated, makes you focus on all the elements necessary to determine corporate strategy, such as internal and external environment, weaknesses, competitive threats, strengths, critical needs for success. It gave us a unified strategy against which we could test our tactics on a day-to-day basis."

"By agreeing to a strategy, you also agree as to what you're *not* going to do. This avoids wasting time and resources on activities that do not support the strategy. Our people became more focused on success and stopped debating alternatives."

Cologne Life Reinsurance Company   GeneralCologne Re.
Mike Magsig
Former CEO

"I think that one of the beauties of what DPI brings to the table is that they don't bring solutions. They bring a process that becomes ours and something we can embody in the normal course of building our organization."

"It brings greater discipline in establishing initiatives, and improving our prioritization. It helps limit the number of initiatives we would be undertaking by helping us really weigh how central they are to the strategy."

"The process has elevated the organization's confidence in being able to continue to produce exceptional results. We have a means of examining the environment, the company, and opportunities in a way that I think can permit us to identify those opportunities much more quickly and cast off pseudo opportunities more quickly and systematically than we could have in the past."

"In terms of our competitive sandbox, we needed to redefine what was going to constitute success for us, and in doing so it led us to a grid-type comparative that we update every few months in terms of our key competitors and where we are with regard to percentage increases and revenue growth and return on equity. What that causes us to do then is to look for certain types of niches and special types of opportunities and certain buying habits of customers that will permit us to retain that positioning on this grid."

"It's not something that is achieved by putting the organization on automatic pilot. It couldn't have been achieved if we had been maintaining a business-as-usual mode. We are giving much more attention, through several critical issue groups, to action plans that are further developing certain of our strengths and permitting us to deploy those better in these niches that we're identifying."

"Critical Issues are a linkage to strategy, to Areas of Excellence, and our strategic guidelines. By pulling all that together under a kind of umbrella of our vision, what this has all done is to sharpen our vision, and it has given more of an implementation orientation to realizing the vision we've created for this company."

Quanex Corporation
Vernon Oechsle
CEO

"I thought our Driving Force was Technology or Production Capacity, and others thought it was Production Capability because we do have unique processing capabilities that allow us to make customized value-added products. I realized early on that they were right and I was wrong, but I hung on because I thought that might solidify them and it would certainly strengthen their reasoning. As I challenged them harder, it made them think about it harder and gave them more conviction that it really was our unique processing capability that is our Driving Force and makes us successful. Eventually I lost. Everybody was delighted that I rolled over. Of course I made a big deal out of it. It was fun."

"I believe, and of course it's been proven, that these DPI people are not consultants in the traditional sense, they're facilitators. And the process is what they offer. It's a wonderful process, and it really works. I think it's so flexible that it can work with a small corporate group, or with the much broader group that we involved. It depends on what the CEO wants to do."

GATX
James Glasser
Chairman of the Board, President & CEO

"The wonderful thing about this process is that a consultant didn't come in and tell us what our strengths and weaknesses are, what we ought to capitalize on, what our Driving Force or strategy should be. The facilitator of the process didn't *tell* us anything. He just kept directing our thinking, asking questions. And the great thing was, he would never give up. Even when we were getting tired or ducking an issue that was unresolved, he wouldn't let us duck. He just kept on directing us to get to a conclusion using this rational process."

"The communication that has developed through this process has great value. Because of it, we're making progress on critical issues that we had tried for a long time to resolve. The DPI Process is not only such a great communication device, but also it is a tool for integrating new thinking and processes in an established culture. Increasing the level and quality of communication is particularly tough to achieve when you're running a holding company. The most beneficial output has been the increased communication and cooperation among our subsidiaries towards improved customer service, employee involvement and satisfaction, and achieving sustainable growth in shareholder value."

D.B. Riley
John Halloran
CEO

"Going through the Strategic Thinking Process, nothing seemed like rocket science, it was just basic and logical. But it really made us think. And you know the questions were very basic. We just kept wondering when the rocket science portion was going to happen, and never got there. It's not rocket science. It's common sense."

"It was quite different than your typical strategic planning. That process has kind of gotten old. In the older strategic planning methods you tend to develop a bunch of paper and you put it in a big bound volume and it sits on a shelf."

Global Marine, Inc.
Russell Luigs
Chairman

"The fact that *you do the thinking yourselves* under the guidance of an experienced facilitator like DPI's Mark Thompson is what makes the difference. The facilitator provides focus and know-how derived from having done it again and again, having previously brought disparate groups through the same process. A facilitator like Mark keeps the process moving, preventing it from going off on non-productive meanders. A very key factor is that the process utilizes the in-depth knowledge of the management team, rather than relying on a quick study by an outsider."

"Basically the process enabled us to sit down with a clean sheet of paper and say 'Ok, what do we want this company to look like and *why*? Further, why *don't* we want it to look like something *else*?' There are really two questions there. Why do you want to do *this*? But, perhaps of more strategic importance is, why do you *not* want to do *that*?"

"There's an old saying that reasonable people, equally informed, seldom disagree. This process goes a long way towards satisfying the equally informed part of that equation."

FLEXcon
Neil McDonough
President

FLEXCON
packaging systems

"The real value in revisiting the strategy on a regular basis through Strategic Thinking is not in changing direction, but in getting our Business Concept more and more refined, understanding our situation better, and developing the list of Critical Issues to bring us closer to that vision that we've got for our future."

"New products are the lifeblood of our company. We put DPI's Strategic Product Innovation Process into place about eighteen months ago. And after eighteen months *30% of our sales come from new products*. We started with a goal of 30% in *three years*. Obviously, we blew that away. Through the first four months of this year, *we came up with 179 products*, using combinations of materials we had never made before. We made *and sold* them. So this has been very successful for us!"

"It all comes down to getting agreement on the Driving Force, and the Business Concept, so that you can develop the Critical Issues from there. It's very straightforward. You've just got to invest the time and do it. And do it with a facilitator who has the experience to force you through these questions and keep the process on track. Then, once you've gotten down to the Critical Issues, give people the tools to make the right decisions and get things done. If you're going to tackle complex issues, you've got to embed these concepts in your company's culture."

"We use DPI's tools for all kinds of operational and strategic decisions. I even used Decision Analysis when we sat down to work out a corporate structure that will enable the company to grow toward our goal of a billion dollars by 2010."

Telepac
Carlos Sousa Alves
CEO

Telepac
Comunicação de Dados

"In fact, during the DPI Strategic Product Innovation Process meeting shared by thirty-five company staff members, extremely well led by René Cordeiro, ninety-two ideas were searched, producing fifty-two opportunities from which we selected to explore twenty-two concepts of new products and services. In the next five years, these new products will result in sales above nineteen billion escudos ($100 million) with costs that will not exceed twelve billion escudos ($63 million). A successful management needs a good forecast."

Héroux, Inc.
Gilles Labbé
Chairman & CEO

"The people who went through this process were not used to being asked to think about the future of the business. Most of the time, they concentrate on operational issues and all of a sudden we were saying, 'Okay, now you have to put another hat on your head, and look at the future direction of the company.' That's not easy for some people to do. But what the process does is allow people to step back and see beyond all the trees to visualize the forest. It was good for us to do. Together we were able to set goals for the company. We decided to grow Héroux at the rate of fifteen percent per year, without taking into account possible acquisitions. And at the end of the first year, our goal was reached. Our stock price had doubled. We have grown at that rate for a couple of years now. Looking ahead, we are confident in achieving a fifteen percent sales growth this year again."

"The strategy is clear. Everyone knows what they have to do in their individual businesses, and we know what we have to do at the corporate level. We have a more focused approach now. Since the process started, the whole company has been changing. The people are changing. We know we have this goal in common. It's not just me in the ivory tower thinking this; it is a shared objective by the people working with me."

"The follow-up that DPI brings is very important to success. Other consultants may come in and put your strategic plan together. But once you're in possession of the plan they're done. They go away and see you again in a year or two. But the DPI people have organized follow-ups in a systematic way. After so many months, we get together with the facilitator and benchmark our progress. 'Where are we? Where are we on each critical issue? Where are we versus where we said we'd be?' "

"The facilitator basically guides us. He doesn't give us the answers. We enter a tunnel. It's very, very wide at first, then narrows down as you go through the process. The facilitator presents the steps, A, B, C, D. Michel Moisan is good at managing us, keeping us in the framework to the final product–a concrete game plan to grow our business. I have only good things to say about DPI. They're a very good organization. They're very serious people. We're happy to work with them."

"No matter what you think, you need to do this. This will change the way you look at your business. This will not only change how *you* look at the future, but also how your key managers do. They will have the same vision you have. This is the key to succeeding."

FirstRand Limited
Laurie Dippenaar
CEO

"At the top we don't have a command and control mentality. We rather see ourselves as being strategic enablers and facilitators. That's the role. Because we feel that, if you really believe in an empowered, autonomous, owner-manager type of culture in your operating company, the only style that fits in well with that at the center is if you style yourself as a strategic enabler and facilitator. We like to think of ourselves as, not a "rule-driven" group, but a "value-driven" group. I explain this to people as follows–Do you want to establish a rule for everything for your children, or do you just want to give them a set of values and then they conduct themselves according to that value system rather than by reference to the rule that father and mother have lain down? This filtered down to all levels and we found ordinary people doing exceptional things."

"In our first exposure to DPI's process we actually used it to get the captains of our different operating units, the CEO's, to arrive at a common understanding of our business philosophy. So, it wasn't really what the DPI process was primarily designed for. We weren't trying to necessarily find our Driving Force as DPI puts it. But we just thought if we go through this process we're going to get a common understanding and buy-in into our business philosophy. And it definitely achieved that objective. Obviously, what's affected us more than anything else is the fact that it systematically extracts the thinking and ideas from the executives' heads, rather than imposing the consultant's thinking. I think it almost *forces* it out of their heads. That obviously leads to the strategy being owned by the company, rather than by the consultant. I'm not just repeating what DPI says, it actually works that way."

"Alignment of thinking is very, very important. And DPI's process is extremely useful for that. You can use it to align thinking within a business unit or you can use it to align thinking within a group of businesses. And it does it very quickly. You can get to the same alignment of thinking over years, but with this, in a matter of days you get there."

"We've never been great users of consultants. Can I just say that it's a credit to DPI that we've used them so extensively? It was partly because the style suits us. We don't want our business run by consultants."

"One of the most valuable contributions to our thinking from the DPI process is that it provides a filter for the opportunities that you're swamped with. You can easily choose the ones that fit strategically so you don't go chasing hares across the plains."

Mail-Well Envelope Division
Luc Desjardins
President & CEO

"We came out of those sessions with a clear action plan as to how we would get the necessary results in plant operations, equipment, management, business unit structures, product development–all of the factors we needed to address to bring us the necessary profitability in a short period of time. And we accomplished that. We not only improved the overall profitability of Supremex, but also added significant profit to the Pac National Group, which was not making money before. In all, we added 7 million dollars in profit in 1997 compared to the 1996 results."

"We were able to achieve fast results, because everybody believed in the strategy and objectives. And they believed they were achievable because we had early successes. So we went on implementing our Critical Issues in every region. The quality of implementation continues to be one of our competitive advantages. We have this outstanding team. They are so good and so fast. The combination of strategy development and strategy deployment is what is different about DPI, and what creates success."

"The excitement now is at a very high level. We can hardly wait for the bottom line to show that this is all working well. It's nice to have a strategy, but 80% of the game is whether you're managing those Critical Issues. DPI gives you a very good follow-up system to make sure they are resolved. We are now on the move to become the leader that we should be in our industry."

Juvena/La Prairie Group
Harald Stolzenberg
President

"We could have easily written down a five page Business Concept, but Marnix Coopman drove us to get it down to a few sentences. When we really condensed it we saw why this part is so important. This is the precise expression of our strategy. It guides us in knowing what we have to do about it."

"One of the advantages of this Process is that the people who were present and those they have spread the word to are taking a more corporate view of where we should go and invest. They now can look at the company as a whole, not just at their own brand. I can say, very clearly, that has happened. That alone was worth the effort."

Bossard Group
Heinrich Bossard
CEO

Bossard

"Actually, DPI's e-Strategy methodology is process oriented without distortion of the content. We weren't, at that point, looking for a particular solution. We were looking for a process to help *us* decide what we wanted the Internet to do for us. DPI's way gave us the opportunity to develop our own e-strategy using their instruments *neutrally*, without bias toward a specific solution. They acted like a metronome. We had to play the piano, but they provided the metronome. They didn't try to impose any solutions. I always watched out for that during the process. I would say DPI managed it well."

"The concept of the *e-nablers* did a lot of things. It really demystified the issues by navigating through the amorphous mass of e-information. Before, we had a kind of a jungle developing. People were saying, 'Have you heard of this, have you heard of that?' People went to seminars, and were saying, 'Why don't we do this or that, everybody else is doing it, why aren't we further along?' And DPI's Process helped us to navigate through that amorphous mass and develop a proper understanding of what we want to do or don't want to do. It gave us the ability to position these *e-nablers* in our minds and have a common understanding of what we are talking about. We can label it and grasp what it is."

FAGOR Electrodomésticos
Jesus Catania
Managing Director

"The most important part of the DPI Strategic Thinking Process is that it draws out the best knowledge of everyone in the room about every aspect of the business. Yet, it does this in a disciplined and objective manner. The DPI facilitator, however, does not allow us to make any false assumptions about ourselves. He challenged and provoked our thinking in a constructive manner."

"Compared to other strategy methods, the DPI process also forces you to explore different scenarios for the future of the business. In other words, Strategic Thinking is not linear in that it doesn't extrapolate the current strategy forward, but causes you to explore different alternatives before choosing the one most appropriate to deal with the environment the business will face in the future rather than the one it faced in the past. If necessary, the new strategy could represent a rupture from the current one if that is what is needed for the company to succeed."

"I would like to say a word about the need for a third party, objective facilitator with a structured process. This role is indispensable. Otherwise the group and the discussion would meander all over the place. A third party facilitator who understands the process better than we do is a better judge of the quality of the answers and ensures that we have not skipped any steps that might lead to wrong conclusions. Furthermore, we have an expression in Spain that says, 'One is never a prophet in one's backyard.' My management is more than likely to be more attentive to an outside person than they would be to me if I attempted to do this myself."

BN/Bombardier Eurorail
Bernard Sorel
Managing Director

"The concepts of Driving Force and Controlling The Sandbox have become part of our modus operandi. Three times (twice at Caterpillar and once at BN), I have noted that the concept of Driving Force in the DPI Process enabled the management team to articulate a clear statement of strategy, clear strategic objectives, and a short list of Critical Issues that allowed the company to manage its resources more effectively. The process helps management to aim its resources at strategic targets, avoiding dispersion and waste of energy."

"It was imperative for us to rally the management team around a new strategy quickly. Furthermore, the presence of an experienced DPI facilitator was indispensable in guiding us through a series of questions in a systematic manner, keeping the debate focused on the essential elements and away from the trivia. This brought us in a short span of time to conclusions that brought quick and tangible results. It would have been impossible to do this on our own."